PRAISE FOR
SUN SHINING ON MORNING SNOW

"*Sun Shining on Morning Snow* is a profound and beautifully told exploration of mixed-race identity, resilience, and belonging. Ingrid Hu Dahl captures the nuanced experience of growing up between cultures with honesty and grace, offering a powerful reminder that being mixed is not about division—it's about the strength of embodying two worlds. A must-read for anyone seeking to understand the complex realities of being mixed and navigating identity in a world that often demands simplicity."

ALEX CHESTER-IWATA, CEO of Mixed Asian Media

"*Sun Shining on Morning Snow* is a visceral look at identity and the harrowing journey so many of us traverse to find belonging. Ingrid Hu Dahl's vivid imagery and unflinching willingness to bare her soul allows us a rare opportunity to see the world through her eyes. Through this lens, we simultaneously see the beauty of our differences and the heartbreaking rejection of those identities within our communities, our families, and even ourselves. This beautifully written book is a must-read portrait of the complexities of being human."

REGINA LAWLESS, author of *Do You*

"*Sun Shining on Morning Snow* isn't just a memoir—it's a heartfelt journey of resilience, identity, and love. As a fellow half-Asian, I saw my own reflections in Ingrid Hu Dahl's story, her words shining with honesty and warmth. She invites readers to laugh, grieve, and grow alongside her, offering a powerful testament to belonging and self-discovery. This book is a gift for anyone seeking a deeper connection to themselves and the world around them. Profoundly moving and beautifully told, it will stay with you long after the final page."

LISA OKADA WHITSITT, founding member of Jilly Bing

"This book is a reflection of the power of being authentic and vulnerable, digging deep into yourself and having the courage to shine your light, even when it feels scary."

SHANTELL MARTIN, British mixed-race artist

SUN
SHINING
ON
MORNING
SNOW

A Memoir of Identity, Loss, and Living Boldly

INGRID HU DAHL

SUN SHINING ON MORNING SNOW

PAGE TWO

Copyright © 2025 by Ingrid Hu Dahl

All rights reserved. No part of this book may be reproduced, stored in a retrieval system or transmitted, in any form or by any means, without the prior written consent of the publisher, except in the case of brief quotations, embodied in reviews and articles.

Some names and identifying details have been changed to protect the privacy of individuals.

Cataloguing in publication information is available from Library and Archives Canada.
ISBN 978-1-77458-617-4 (paperback)
ISBN 978-1-77458-618-1 (ebook)

Page Two
pagetwo.com

Page Two™ is a trademark owned by Page Two Strategies Inc., and is used under license by authorized licensees

Cover and interior design by Taysia Louie
Cover illustration by Hanna Barczyk
All photos courtesy of the author

ingridhudahl.com

For Ma Bao Bei
媽寶貝

To what can human life be likened?
Consider, perhaps, a tiny bird in winter
That alights for a fleeting moment
On the morning snow
And then flies away, without any thought
That the footprints she leaves behind
Will soon be gone,
Erased by the blowing wind

SU SHI, "Recalling Minchi with My Brother Ziyou"

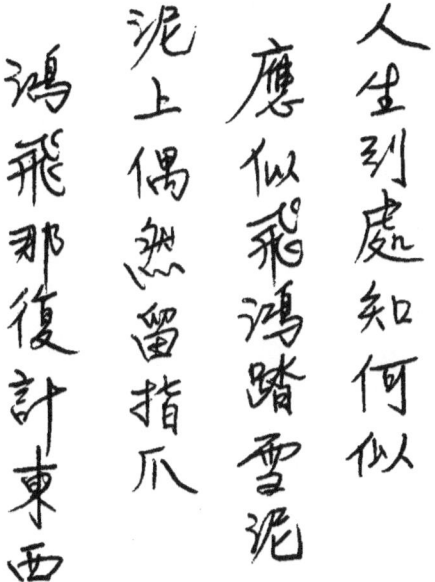

Ma's handwritten version of Su Shi's poem that Ba saw on her dorm wall.

CONTENTS

一 HELLO, WORLD *1*

二 MIXED-BLOOD CHILD *31*

三 EQUESTRIAN BARN RAT *55*

四 ALL THE HUNGRY WOLVES *83*

五 TWISTED IN DESIRE *109*

六 SWALLOW THE MIC *145*

七 RAGE AGAINST THE STAGE *173*

八 MORE THAN A WOMAN *201*

九 QUARANTINE DIARIES *239*

十 THE PHOENIX *269*

ACKNOWLEDGMENTS *287*

AUTHOR'S NOTE *291*

HELLO, WORLD

I ENTERED THIS WORLD demanding to see who was in charge. In the middle of the birth canal, I got tangled up in the umbilical cord. My heart stopped beating. There was panic in the delivery room. My mom had been in labor for more than forty hours. Doctors considered an emergency C-section. Even at the young age of twenty-four, my mother had exhausted all her energy. But to everyone's surprise, my heartbeat revived. Hovering in the membrane separating life and death, my warrior spirit wrestled me free and out I came, screaming with my entire life force.

I wasn't handed into the comforting arms of my mother. I was whisked away. My father was asked for my name. He and my mother were told they were having a boy up until the moment I was born. The only name they came prepared with was "Jonathan," which they ended up saving for my future little brother. I remained unnamed for three days until my white grandma came up with "Ingrid"—a nod to my father's Scandinavian background.

My parents added "Samantha" as my middle name, inspired by their favorite character from the American fantasy sitcom *Bewitched*, where a witch marries an ordinary man. I love that my middle name was connected to a character who, despite her special powers and vibrant family, had to navigate bi-species limitations living as a mortal in order to be with the person she loved.

Like my own mother, Samantha birthed a mixed kid—half witch, half human. But in our non-fantasy series, my parents lived with real cultural and racial challenges and backlash, requiring them to stand up for their love and one another, as well as their offspring. They navigated harsh assumptions—for my Ba, that he had "picked up Mom" while serving in the army or that he had a sexual fetish for Asian, servitude-inclined women. For my Ma, that she was simply seeking a green card or that she was a "gold digger" seeking a white knight. Neither could be further from the truth. And truth is the raison d'être for this book.

Having "Samantha" as a middle name was short lived. Once word got to my nai nai in Taiwan that my name didn't reflect my Chinese heritage, "Samantha" and all its romanticism was crossed off my birth certificate and the powerful "Hu" name took its rightful place. Hello, world, I'm not a boy, nor a warlock, but the first mixed-race girl in my family: Ingrid Hu Dahl.

I WAS A BIG BABY: eight pounds and nine ounces barreling through my mom's petite and lean five-foot-five body. I was a hungry infant. I drank all the formula I was given with a thirst that surprised many—a thirst that would match my boldness to come.

My parents Hu Kuo-Ying—who introduced herself as Kuo-Ying Judy Hu in graduate school until she became Judy Hu Dahl—and Nathaniel Harald Dahl had married just nine months prior to my arrival. They met and fell in love in April 1978. Ma was in her second semester at Rutgers University as a student in the Graduate School of Library and Information Studies. Ba was an undergrad sophomore taking courses in science and theatre arts.

They met twice—once at the international table on campus to mingle and the second time on a double date where Dad was Mom's roommate's date. He walked into their dorm room, admiring a framed artwork of a famous Chinese poem, "Recalling Minchi with My Brother Ziyou" by Su Shi from the Song Dynasty:

To what can human life be likened?
Consider, perhaps, a tiny bird in winter
That alights for a fleeting moment
On the morning snow
And then flies away, without any thought
That the footprints she leaves behind
Will soon be gone,
Erased by the blowing wind

My father asked my mom to translate the characters, which she recited in her heavy accent. He was moved. Not just by the poem, but also by the depth of feeling in her confident words. This led them to speaking for several hours about the meaning of life, their hopes for the future, and what was important to them—which had striking similarities.

As they walked and talked after their respective dates had long left, my dad felt like pinching himself to make

Hello, world,
I'm not a boy, nor a
warlock, but the
first mixed-race girl
in my family:
Ingrid Hu Dahl.

sure he wasn't dreaming. The thought of this beautiful, amazing woman sharing such things with him, and what that meant, was too good to be true. He was in the clouds and didn't want to come back to earth, ever. That night he wrote in his journal: *I think tonight I've met the most wonderful girl in the world.* From that day on, his whole life took a new direction. Miraculously to Dad, Mom seemed to have romantic feelings for him, too—and he could hardly believe it! This sparked their profound love story and an unflinching desire to be wed.

Not everyone saw the magic in my parents' match. At least, not right away. Both sets of families were startled, even shocked, by the interracial match. Ma was Taiwanese, of Chinese descent; Ba was American, of European and Scandinavian descent. Family members questioned the different races at play and how that would impact them.

Back in Taipei, Taiwan, my mother's family referred to Dad as a "white barbarian." That summer, my mom was asked to come back to Taipei. Her parents wanted to persuade her to return to the track that they had charted for her, one that aligned with their cultural expectations. They hoped she would rekindle feelings for her previous boyfriend because he met with their approval, even if he was a real jerk. Mom's grandmother, Zhong Shou-Yi, was married to a judge and former president of the Supreme Court of the Republic of China. Due to the high number of orphans among those killed during the Second Sino-Japanese War and the Communist Revolution, Zhong Shou-Yi started an orphanage that would eventually relocate from China to Taiwan. My grandfather, Hu Tong-Sheng, the son of a senator, met and married Zhong Shou-Yi's daughter, my grandmother Hu Lee Shi Mei, an educated leader who would run the Taipei-based family orphanage, Yi Kuang. Given the strong family lineage, they expected Mom to follow in their footsteps.

Every day, Mom's parents watched as she wrote letters to my dad and received daily responses in the mail from him in the US. They watched as Mom awaited pricey, long-distance phone calls, week after week. They saw her tears and the gravitational pull she felt to be back with the man she loved. That summer, Ba learned enough Mandarin to communicate with Ma's family and explain to them his intention to marry their daughter and his commitment to being her forever-ever. He planned to fly to Taipei and worked three jobs to raise the funds to do so. But before he bought the ticket, something miraculous happened. My grandparents put aside their concerns about Ma's cross-continental love affair with a "barbarian" and gave them their blessing. The Bee Gees song "If I Can't Have You" was my parents' love song. It's not hard to see why. The lyrics speak to the loneliness and yearning for a love that requires tremendous effort. It was a time of bliss.

MA RETURNED TO THE STATES for her fall term. She continued her studies and married Ba that spring. They wed in a ceremony witnessed by friends, professors, siblings, and nearby relatives. Photos from their wedding brought two families together. My parents are beaming in the pictures, all smiles, with their small group of attendees. Ma wore a white dress and veiled, brimmed sun hat. Ba wore a bluish-gray suit. Ma held a small bouquet of flowers, and in one picture, she's admiring the topper of their two-layer cake. Their victorious love was just the tip of the iceberg. Little did they know that nine months later, the first mixed-race child of the family would enter center stage. Me.

When I entered the world in 1980, interracial marriage had been legal in the US for only thirteen years. That year, the US census reported only 3 percent of married couples were from different racial groups. My parents' love required resilience. Racism and sexism held firmly to the surface of the bubble they occupied. Passersby did not hide their dismay at their open affection. My parents' truth—their love—was an act of bravery, a declaration of sorts, but also one that would always have a spotlight. Their life together would be a spectacle, open to ridicule, envy, and unwanted glares and judgmental gazes coming from all directions—even from those closest to them.

As a young couple, they pushed aside these pressures with a bravery I admire. Their courage anchored me as the *first* of the family's next generation—and the first hapa at that. I respectfully use the term "hapa," a term that originally comes from the Hawaiian phrase "hapa haole," meaning "half white."

Although no one referred to me as "mixed race" or "hapa" as a child, being the first hapa family member is of great importance to me. The mixing of race, culture, and language would be a part of our lives from here on out.

AS SHE RECOVERED from giving birth, Ma chose a Chinese name for her new baby girl: "Tao Xue-Qing," written as 陶雪晴 in Chinese. She chose "Tao" as our Chinese American family name because it was an approximate transliteration of Ba's Scandinavian surname "Dahl." Ma associated her little baby girl with the pure and delicate beauty of newly fallen snow. Years later, she would describe the meaning of my name as the sun shining on the morning snow after a storm passed, its glittery landscape sparkling like crystals. I love my name: sun shining on morning snow.

My parents returned from Saint Peter's University Hospital in New Brunswick, New Jersey, to their humble lodgings: married student housing on Rutgers-Busch campus. Their apartment was a tiny, basic space with painted cinder-block walls, linoleum floors, and a cockroach infestation—but my parents loved their first home together. They bought used furniture and happily accepted hand-me-downs. They connected with their dynamic neighbors, a friendly mix of students who pursued degrees with their spouses in tow.

When my parents found out they were pregnant, they applied for an upgrade, given that married students with children qualified for better digs. These apartments were newer, larger, and had air conditioning for the hot New Jersey summers. When I arrived, my parents moved us into our new apartment, where we lived for the next three years. During that time, my young parents worked hard to finish their degrees while raising me and looked at career opportunities in software and computer science. There were times of singing and dancing, and times of quiet when studying commenced. Ma finished her first master's degree in library and information studies and was encouraged by her mother to get a second master's in computer science with a focus on artificial intelligence.

Once my dad became a father, he transitioned from the gigs of his youth—working on a local farm, pumping gas, and the like—into adulthood with an office job. Both my parents got jobs in software engineering. Ba found a job through a chance encounter at a career-fair training program. Ma had an advantage with her master's degree. She was laying the foundation for what she would later become—a tech pioneer in mobility.

I am still surprised that no one has documented my mom's exceptional, sought-after leadership qualities and her inventive ability to think into the future and design software to meet consumer demands. Later, when I was in my early twenties, Ma shared her vision of the future, telling me that technology would be controlled in the palm of your hand. Our phones would turn on our TVs and lower our window blinds. I struggled to follow. I remember asking her, "Ma, why would people want that?" And she looked at me with her eyes bright towards the future: "They don't know they want that yet. But they will."

To be clear, Ma wasn't a stereotypical tech nerd. She was a fashionista, a total babe, a brilliant thinker, and a dreamer. She was complex. She somehow balanced being a creative—scribbling in her journal on weekends, capturing dreams, poetry, and ideas that mattered to her—while navigating the rigidity of the corporate world and the demands of her growing, devout Christianity. She became the family breadwinner who traveled the world and drank whiskey sours on business trips, while Ba sang and danced in the kitchen, making dinner after he got home from work.

EVERY OTHER YEAR or so, we would get the opportunity to fly to Taipei, Taiwan, and visit Nai Nai and family. I loved these trips. It was another world! My family in Taipei had hired help who would take me out with them on their errands. As a child, I rode on the back of scooters without a helmet, the wind whipping at my face as we sped through the busy city streets. At every turn, a new scene or scent came and went. We whizzed past delicious street food being sold by vendors. At red lights, I'd watch people on sidewalks bartering for the best price on produce or counterfeit clothing, one of my personal faves.

These trips infused my life with color and instilled in me a taste for adventure, culture, and language. Chinese—its visual descriptors, imagery, and tones—was lodged in my brain. Chinese was my first language, followed by English, and at home we spoke a mix of the two: Chinglish. Mandarin is a tonal language with four specific tones. When spoken, each word must be pronounced with the correct tone. If you get the tone mixed up, what you say could have a radically different meaning from what you intended. The written Chinese language is made up of visual pictures, displays of characters in action. When I was a child, Ma would explain each character to me in detail, how each partition of strokes displayed a scene of characters and actions. I was enamored with her descriptions. Each stroke came to life on the page as a story, one that my imagination expanded tenfold into a colorful world.

In Taipei, Ma would spend time getting a new hairstyle, upcycling her fashion, and, without missing a beat, hitting up her favorite bakeries. Each time she entered these bakeries, she would close her eyes and take in a whiff of the scents she rarely smelled back in New Jersey. She'd pick up a tray and tongs, slowly examine each display case of bread with cream or pork floss, and eventually move towards the cakes and sweets.

There'd always be plain, sliced mian bao beautifully wrapped as a square loaf—fluffy, sweet, delightful. But Ma gravitated to her favorite: the egg tart. I'd watch her eyes widen as she locked in on this treat, which instilled in me the idea that desserts and precious moments of indulgence are worth savoring.

Taipei, the vibrant city that it is, made everything accessible by foot, car, subway, and, of course, scooter. Unlike her family, who had cars and were driven by chauffeurs or the occasional taxi, Ma preferred to get around by taking public transportation. I didn't mind how we traversed the city because Taipei provided so much that I enjoyed. To this day, I love walking and exploring the city, eating street food, discovering new side streets with hidden treasures, and filling up on stationery-store finds.

As a young child, I didn't feel different in Taipei. I took little notice of the attention I received for my mixed appearance. I couldn't always understand what people said. At this point in my young life, I felt incredibly free. Free to observe and take part in the world. Free to go fast on a scooter in a city that was part of who I was and where my mother came from. Ma and her city were magical.

NAI NAI was the matriarch of the family. She was tall, had a nice figure and a big round face with blown-out hair that always reminded me of a lion's mane. She was incredibly confident and loud like a commander. When she laughed, I thought maybe an earthquake had struck because everything shook around her.

Nai Nai gave me love and shared her expectations for me as the firstborn. In return, I gave her what she coined "the best-quality heart" and care. I made her laugh. She taught me how to play mahjong, and she took me on various outings that were on her agenda. Sometimes we'd go to a museum and look at modern art. Nai Nai soaked up the visual arts. She took me to Chinese opera, high tea, and, of course, shopping, which was one of the ways she expressed herself. She always walked so fast in long strides I could barely keep up with her. Often, my job was to hold her purse or jacket. I was her favorite coatrack.

A few times a week, Nai Nai would get her hair or nails done at a nearby salon, often with one of her two daughters joining her. Everyone paid attention to her magnetic force. She was sassy, classy, and whip-smart. I felt like she ran the city. She was meticulous about money and her financial accounts and generously handed out red envelopes to family and those in need.

I watched her run Yi Kuang and saw how she cared for and housed children who were given up for adoption. Many were shockingly found in trash cans, abandoned due to their intellectual or physical developmental differences. These young babies and children saw her as their mother. I remember admiring her and wishing I could be more involved in her world. Even when one of the kids flipped me the middle finger during my visit. I'll never know if it was jealousy or what, but that moment stayed with me. How innocent we are as children until pain, perceptions of difference, and heightened emotions are in play.

In Taiwan during our visits, all family members were expected to attend dinner at Nai Nai's home most nights. She had taught her hired help how to make her favorite dishes for breakfast, lunch, and dinner. I tried to sneak into the small kitchen to learn these recipes and help clean up, but I was always shooed out. In this environment, I was to be waited on and served—which felt awkward to me, compared to the middle-class American life I lived back home.

I can still hear Nai Nai applauding me back in Taipei every time I'd get up for a second helping of rice. "Tian fan!" she'd roar from deep within her diaphragm (meaning "getting seconds"). She loved how I ate. Taking a second helping acknowledged the cook's talents and the meal's degree of deliciousness. "Tian fan" is often confused with the idiom "tian fan di fu," which translates to "sky and the earth turning upside down." Although my two worlds were halfway around the world from each other, I always felt the sky was right side up. After applauding tian fan, Nai Nai would hum a tune with the most important post-meal tool in hand: the toothpick. Mom lovingly called me "fan tong," meaning "rice bucket." I am a rice bucket.

After dinner, a plate of fresh-cut fruits and toothpicks occupied the adults who remained seated at the table with various glasses of tea or whiskey. I hung out with my younger cousins, speaking broken Chinese and English—whichever was more successful in our communication. I wondered about their lives and how different our experiences were. My American upbringing and my mixed-race identity were never mentioned in our conversations. However, the adults talked about it. I learned years later that my uncle, the middle child, argued with Nai Nai over her estate. He said that even if I was the firstborn of the next generation, as a mixed-blood American grandchild, I wasn't a true Hu. She responded, "She is my grandchild. She *is* a Hu." Thanks, Nai Nai.

Nai Nai was fierce and ran a no-bullshit, my-way-or-the-highway household. If you said or did something she did not approve of, her wrath would follow. She could tell someone off so cuttingly that there'd be nothing left of them afterwards. And yet, she still had so much power in her laughter, you'd wish earplugs were within reach. I rarely had heated arguments with Nai Nai. Most of the time when we got into disagreements, I was older and protecting Ma. Ma was often the recipient of Nai Nai's blame and harsh words. It was an echo from her childhood. Ma grew up with only two school uniforms and nothing else of her own. There were moments when she was slapped for having feelings. Although I never witnessed physical violence, there was a strong undertone of verbal abuse in the family. Sometimes this was directed at my parents or other family members, but rarely at Mom's youngest sister.

My aunt Nancy was Nai Nai's favorite, even though Ma was the eldest. Nancy was a film star, singer, and model who had a master's degree in finance. She was on billboards all over Taiwan. She would go on to become a chief financial officer and investor in several start-ups. Once, when I was three or four years old, paparazzi captured her walking with me in the city, which made the press wonder if I was potentially *her* mystery child. The story showed up in the papers the next day.

Nancy had the ideal relationship with Nai Nai. They would sit for hours at the circular dinner table, laughing and talking, leaving Mom the outsider, always wanting. I watched as my mom, a radiant figure in my life who would often say, "Don't let the bastards get you down," immediately became quiet and small. I called upon my fierce warrior spirit to protect my mom and to make sure she felt loved. But my efforts didn't always work and often went unnoticed.

The only time Nai Nai and I got into a major altercation was later in my teen years when she visited us for the summer. Every day, she made us fried rice after school, which was lovely until we got sick of it. I was yearning for spaghetti with meat sauce, which we often had as a family. But when Nai Nai visited, it seemed she wanted to eat only Chinese food. One morning, I announced that I'd be making dinner: spaghetti with meat sauce. I asked Nai Nai to forgo making her fried rice, which was perhaps surprising coming from a rice bucket like me. I drove home from school, picturing a delicious Italian meal that I'd make within minutes. Unfortunately, when I entered the kitchen Nai Nai had in fact made fried rice, seemingly ignoring my request. I felt I had been a dutiful granddaughter but my simple ask wasn't considered. And so, I blew up and yelled, "Nai Nai, I told you I was going to make dinner tonight!"

Ma watched in the background as my unexpected reaction shocked my grandmother. Nai Nai's face changed red-hot, as if she was igniting an anger bomb in response. Her eyes closed tightly, she shook her head like a lion, and spat out, "You *must* respect me!" It was the loudest, most demanding roar that I had ever heard come out of her.

In that moment, I saw a woman who had to leave her home and family to flee from the Chinese Communist Revolution as a teenager, risking her life to immigrate to Taiwan. I saw her rub dirt on her face, bind her breasts, and sew what little money she had, along with important documents, into her clothes to avoid being robbed or raped, forced into the sex trade, or murdered. I saw a woman who was betrayed by her husband, who kept a secret family and died of a heart attack on his way to tell her the truth. The secret was revealed at the funeral when the second wife and her three children showed up. I saw the effect of that release on her face, body, and energy.

She calmed herself, opened her watery eyes, and looked around, as if seeing with a new lens. I went up to her and sat at her feet to apologize. I let her know she was loved and respected, always. She started to murmur that it was my ma's fault for bringing me up so poorly. It was a mild effort on her part to nurse her ego as she darted blame towards my mom.

"Nai Nai, this is not about Ma. This is this not her fault," I said.

Nai Nai looked up at me and I knew she agreed. As her oldest grandchild, I rushed to her aid whenever she needed it. And this time, I was present with her during this moment of awareness. Sitting at the dinner table, she, Ma, and me—three generations of warrior spirits—shared

Nai Nai, Ma, and I—
three generations of
warrior spirits—shared
the need to be seen,
valued, respected, and,
most importantly, loved.

something we could all agree on: our need to be seen, valued, respected, and, most importantly, loved.

One year, when I was still a toddler and Ma was bringing me back to the US from a solo trip to Taipei, she got held up in customs with our luggage. Ba was waiting for us among a sea of people in the arrival hall at Newark International Airport. Everyone was eager with the anticipation of seeing family and loved ones. The door finally opened but Ba didn't see anyone. Slowly, heads started moving, all eyes fixed on a spot down the arrivals hall. He respectfully pushed through the crowd and saw what had caught their attention: a toddler walking by herself. And not just any toddler, but his daughter! I walked down the hallway, enjoying a bag of shrimp chips, looking at the crowd as if this was just another fashion runway in a different city.

He started waving and shouting, "Ingrid! Ingrid! *Innnnnngrid!*" I didn't hear him. I calmly and confidently continued, every now and then pausing to say "poka" in declaration of my chips. Shortly after, Ma exited the doors, tired yet stunning with her new hairstyle and bold outfit. She followed behind me without a sense of urgency. I picture Ba turning to see her, his babe of a wife walking in slow motion to one of their favorite Bee Gee songs, "More Than a Woman."

Ba was in for it. Not only did he have a stunning wife, but he also had a young, headstrong kid who commanded the space she occupied, even in the presence of a thousand stares. Unfazed, I knew I belonged in this world. Every step I took was without hesitation. The young version of me had a sense of liberation and confidence that I would yearn for in the years to come.

AT THE AGE OF SIX, I first witnessed Ma's confidence getting hard knocked. It was an ordinary day and, at first, just another shopping trip to the Asian grocery store. As usual, my parents split up when we arrived, getting items they had discussed as I wandered, gravitating towards a new item that caught my eye on the lower level. In this case, a stack of unfrozen popsicles wrapped in plastic pastel tubes got me curious about the flavors—pale white was likely lychee or coconut; the pink, dragon fruit or guava. I was debating whether to find one of my parents and ask for their opinion. Maybe we'd add the popsicles to their shopping baskets and give them a try. It was springtime and unusually hot out, and I imagined what a treat a frozen lychee popsicle would be. Chinese music was playing on the loudspeaker.

I looked up and saw Ma at the top of the stairs. I knew she had gone right to the bakery and saw the evidence in a plastic bag she held in her hand—two egg tarts. Ma was seven months pregnant with my baby brother and having one of those hankerings for an indulgence to savor, a reminder of home. I started picturing how much I'd enjoy watching her eat them. Probably she'd eat one during the car ride home to our new house in Belle Mead, New Jersey, and the other after dinner. But the egg tarts didn't make it.

Ma took two steps and slipped, falling bum first down the remaining stairs. She landed with her legs spread awkwardly underneath her. Her huge belly looked like the weight of the whole world had pushed her down the staircase. The music was the only thing I could hear until my father started shouting "JUDY!" over the volume. I watched in terror and shock. I was frozen momentarily before I, too, ran over. I noticed that there were many people in the store. All Asian. No one went to help my beautiful, pregnant mother. I looked around, wondering what kept them from running to her. They just watched as Ba ran to her side. Their expressions were odd—as if my parents had done something they disapproved of. *What is wrong with everyone?* I wondered.

I was by Ma's side with Ba, ready to help her up.

"Ma! Are you okay?! Are you hurt?"

"Jude?" Dad put his arms around her waist to help lift her up. "Jude, are you okay?"

His voice was suddenly a whisper, instead of the shout of his initial shock. It was as if he could feel all the onlookers' eyes boring into the back of his head. He hovered over her, to protect her from the unwanted stares.

I looked at Ma's face. Her cheeks were rosy with embarrassment. She looked down at the floor, which didn't make sense. She *fell*. She did nothing wrong! As she began to prop herself up, she shifted her weight and pulled the small plastic bag of squished egg tarts out from under her.

"I ruined the tarts" was all she said, quietly, as if she was a child admitting to some wrongdoing, not the dangerous fall she had just experienced as a pregnant woman.

I looked around me at the mix of averted and staring eyes, and I understood. Even at age six, it was clear: the tarts belonged more than we did.

IT WASN'T JUST instances like the one at the Asian grocery store where we were treated like outsiders. It happened even with our own families.

My white grandma, whom I called "Gram," cooked, sewed, and drove with a lead foot. Riding with her in the car was always a matter of survival; you had to remind her to look at the road because if something caught her eye on the horizon, she'd get distracted. At an early age, I saw her as an independent woman and my protector, especially from what she called "spider crickets."

What I didn't know was that Gram was a survivor. She had grown up during the Depression in a poor and abusive household in a family of six children. She was pulled out of school in the eighth grade and expected to work and hand her paychecks to her father. During wrestling or tickling sessions between me and my dad, Gram would often let out a tight breath, put her hands over her eyes, and whimper, "Please stop." Gram had experienced painful things in her youth. She had a deviated septum in her nose. When I was older, I asked her about it and her response was "My father broke it."

Gram was fortunate to have met and married my grandpa in 1949 when she was twenty-six. He was ten years older and in a position to liberate her from her home life. He taught her how to drive a car and balance a checkbook. He built a house in Towaco, New Jersey, for them to move into. Gram was a looker and Grandpop was smitten, not realizing the support she'd need and mental health challenges she would face living as a housewife and mother of three.

Grandpop ran a successful, homegrown art appraisal company in New York City. As a younger man, he started off as a sculptor and part-time bike messenger, which taught him how to navigate the city like the back of his hand. He had served as part of a special unit called the Ghost Army during World War II—a secret operation deployed in Europe to create fake tanks and play recorded tracks of sizeable units to deceive the enemy. It was a success. Thanks to the talented group of artists, actors, performers, and fashion designers—many of whom were gay—they helped save thousands of lives.

Over the holidays, Grandpa hosted a few Ghost Army friends who added flair and fashion to the occasion. My grandpop had an open mind, which he modeled to my father and his two older siblings. Unfortunately, at the young age of fifty-eight, Grandpop had an aneurysm after dropping off a friend at the Princeton train station. As his friend turned to wave goodbye, he saw my grandpa hunched over the steering wheel in the driver's seat. He was rushed to the hospital and, a few days later, died. My father was only fourteen.

Widowed at forty-eight, Gram didn't have any training on how to run the art appraisal business she inherited. It withered and became a shadow of what Grandpop had built. Gram relied on the radio for information. She was depressed and uncertain about her future. She fell into old habits she'd learned during the Depression, like ignoring expiration dates and wiping mold off of food to make it palatable. She'd say, "Oh, that's still alright."

Whenever we went over to Gram's house, after a brief welcome, Ma was notorious for beelining it to Gram's pantry and pulling out all the cans that had expired. Exasperated, Gram would say that they were "still alright" and ask her to leave them be. I was surprised by the pantry and how, without fail, newly expired cans appeared every time we visited—which was often.

I knew that Gram did not particularly support my father and mother's marriage. She had a strained relationship with Nai Nai. They had an obvious language and culture barrier. But it was more than that. Whenever Nai Nai visited the United States, there was always tension between her and Gram. They both seemed to disrespect one another. Perhaps Nai Nai looked down on Gram's lack of education and leaned on classism to distinguish her rank. Whiteness provided Gram with her own racial currency. I noticed the strange way she looked at Nai Nai, but, as a kid, I didn't recognize or understand it. I now know it as racism.

One day, Gram became increasingly animated while watching something on TV. I don't recall what was airing—but she was emotionally charged. She was taking short, rapid gasps and saying things under her breath. Her entire tone and energy shifted to anger, spite, and exasperation.

I looked up at the screen and saw Asian people. Even as a young kid under the age of ten, I spoke up: "Gram, what are you saying?"

She retorted a lot of angry words about people of color. I didn't understand everything she said but could feel the power of its undertone. Her voice was righteous, full of blame, a one-way directness that lacked any curiosity or interest in relating to the people on the other side of the screen.

"Gram, *those* people are *me*," I said, confronting her.

"You're *not* them, Ingrid!" she said in an exasperated tone, as if I'd taken the Lord's name in vain. "You're *my* granddaughter."

I looked at her and, from a deep sense of self, I said definitively: "I am your granddaughter. And I am them."

A tiny shift happened in both of us that day. Years went by and I never heard her say racist things in that way again. I realized that racism was not something my family members had been spared from. They were in it, too; everyone in the world had been taught, seduced, and blinded by racism. "Tian fan di fu," the Chinese idiom that sounded like the words for rice bucket, suddenly came into play—the sky and the earth turning upside down.

THE FIRST PERSON I ever saw on TV who looked like me was another Samantha: Sam Micelli, played by the actress Alyssa Milano in the show *Who's the Boss?* The series was important for me to witness because it centered on a feisty, bold, confident, and independent tomboy full of optimism and curiosity about life. Even though Alyssa Milano is not mixed race, her appearance was the closest I had ever seen to a mixed-race girl in the media. Her closeness to her father and respect for the matriarchs in the house was comforting. My parents hoped that given how popular Milano was and how we looked alike that I might "fit in" better with my peers.

At that time, representation of diverse people was extremely limited and gender roles stuck to a social script my family didn't prescribe to. As a child, I was aghast when I saw Disney's interpretation of interbreed mixing in *Lady and the Tramp*, considered an endearing animated musical when it was made in 1955. At the end of the movie, the two very distinct dog breeds—American cocker spaniel and schnauzer-shepherd—have a litter of puppies that are mini versions of each breed, gendered according to their mom and dad. Now, when two different purebred or mixed dogs have puppies, the resulting litter tends to have a wide range of mixed combinations. Perhaps the designers lacked the imagination to create a mixed-breed litter, but Disney just made carbon copies. I found this startling and shortsighted.

In contrast, when, at age seven, I was introduced to sci-fi through the TV series *Star Trek: The Next Generation* (*TNG*), the genre expanded my imagination beyond our world—think of the possibilities out there in the universe, where there are all kinds of difference to encounter!

On Sunday evenings, between 1987 and 1994, my family and I would wait for the new episode of *TNG* to air on television. The show offered more diversity in gender and racial representations as the starship explored "strange, new worlds." Captain Jean-Luc Picard represented a kind of leadership that resonated with me. He was thoughtful, considered the input of his entire team, and actively sought advice of a female counselor, the empath Deanna Troi. Beverly Crusher was the physician, and Geordi La Forge was the lead engineer. *TNG* introduced us to a place no one had gone before—a place where there weren't just men or white people, but all of us. During the series, audiences were introduced to androgynous characters with a fundamental respect and dignity that my family and I rarely experienced because we were seen as different.

Sir Patrick Stewart, the actor who played Captain Picard, captured Whoopi Goldberg's sentiment about *TNG*'s impact on people of color in his memoir *Making It So*: "*Star Trek*, in its different incarnations, present[s] an aspirational future preferable to our present—a future where inclusivity is a given rather than an effort." That inclusive future was what I craved as a hapa kid. The stories, experiences, and roles we cast must reflect those we embody in reality. I was hungry for a future that was different from the limitations of my present.

top My parents, young and in love.
bottom My parents and I soon after I entered the world.

Summertime in New Jersey with Ma.

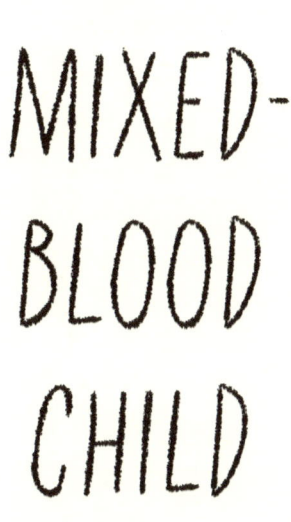

MIXED-BLOOD CHILD

"**H**ALF PIECE OF SHIT," the popular fifth-grade boy called me on a cold fall morning. I was in first grade, minding my own business at the bus stop. I noticed that the other kids stood quietly nearby, saying nothing. I looked down at my outfit, searching for a reason I had been addressed. Nothing unusual. A purple puffy coat and white sneakers with ruffled socks. I was holding a My Little Pony lunchbox, and my chin-length black hair was pulled behind my ears. I looked at the boy's face. It was so twisted in disgust he almost appeared sick or poisoned. I wondered, *Am I in danger?*

As a first grader, swear words weren't a part of my vernacular but I knew "shit" wasn't a good word. The way he said it was spiteful and angry, as if we had some long history of knowing one another and I had committed a cutting betrayal. *What did I do? Why did he call me that?* I wondered. Had he meant to call someone else that? *Why me?* I looked around. I felt eerily exposed, misunderstood, and unwelcomed. There was no dialogue to be had, no offering to engage. I stood there as the energy of his name-calling hovered over me. A chill crept into my throat. I had noticed my parents experiencing strange reactions from people in town, but this morning was different. The spotlight was directed at me.

The chill in my throat was met with a warm sensation rising in my spine. As if the two strands of my DNA were wrapped in different temperatures, exposing this split in my identity, cut yet balanced in half. I filed this encounter somewhere in my psyche, away from my parents and family, so that it might not touch or harm them.

AT THE AGE OF FOUR, my family moved to a predominantly white, suburban development with cookie-cutter houses in central New Jersey. Nai Nai had gifted my parents $50,000 with a written agreement that, in exchange, she could visit and live with my parents whenever she pleased for however long.

Our pale gray house with blue shutters and a two-car garage—which felt like a palace to me—was located on a cul-de-sac. Behind our house was farmland and a few acres of woods. A paved path, which could be navigated by bike or foot, connected the cul-de-sac to other sections of the neighborhood and, most importantly, to the bus stop. Just beyond the bus stop sat an artificial pond, where Ba and I would catch and release rainbow fish under a weeping willow tree.

After completing kindergarten, I was now taking the bus with a range of grade school–aged kids to the local elementary school. I wasn't entirely interested in engaging with the other kids in the neighborhood. I was in my own world and kept to myself. This started from day one of kindergarten. I cried when my parents dropped me off. After they left, the teacher slapped me on the cheek and demanded I stop crying. I was shocked, and my crying abruptly came to an end. I moved as far away from the teacher as I could. Two blonde girls were playing with toys and I thought I might join them. As I walked towards them, the teacher stomped over and pulled me away from them.

"*They* are playing with those toys. You can't until they're done."

I don't even know if the girls took notice, but I can still feel the teacher's grip on my arm. As if my existence affected her personally. I grew increasingly silent. School was a danger zone where adults could harm you. Ma and Ba picked up on my demeanor and soon after, I was attending another kindergarten class.

The next teacher I experienced was warm and kind. It was clear she cared for her students, enjoyed her role as an educator, and treated each of us equally. But she was the exception, as future teachers and specialists seemed to interpret my bilingual skills as a learning disability. This reminded me of my first day at preschool. My parents, anxious and pressed for time, arrived in their corporate suits, holding a piece of paper. It contained a code for translating what I spoke best: Chinglish. What my parents were offering the teacher was a guide for understanding an intimate mix of languages—an insider's view to how we spoke, translating key phrases and their meanings.

"'Xiao bian' means she has to pee-pee," Ma explained.

"'Wo ele' means she is hungry," Ba continued.

The preschool teacher shifted her weight as if she wanted to pee-pee in her pants. This was a new experience the teacher didn't seem prepared for. I wondered, *Do none of the other preschoolers speak a mix of languages like me?*

After a pause, the teacher looked at the phonetics on the page. "Show-bien?" she asked. Ma looked dismayed. She glanced at Ba. He encouraged the teacher to try sounding out the second phrase. She attempted, "Woah... ugh-luh?" I laughed believing that preschool would be hilarious.

Now I was in first grade, my bilingual gifts led me into rooms filled with misfit kids—all boys. They were rowdy and smart, often talking back and rebelling against things. As the sole female, I observed the energy they held. Teachers seemed to find these boys troublesome, even dangerous. I never really knew why I was placed in that crowd. Maybe my dual languages felt dangerous to them, too.

What I found most confusing was the negative attention I received throughout the years—year after year—around my writing abilities. My teachers' written feedback on my papers expressed a similar sentiment: I didn't have the right command of English; I used too much imagery and analogy; and I mixed up words and meaning in a way that was hard to follow. Worst of all, they said I used improper sentence structures and misunderstood common vocabulary. I loved to use words based on how they *sounded*, instead of on their actual definitions, especially if the correct meaning seemed counterintuitive in my mind. Time and time again I was told I wasn't a good writer. This message was repeated throughout my entire schooling and early career, which is fascinating since here I am, writing a book.

When the boy at the bus stop called me "half piece of shit," however, it wasn't a misuse of language. It was clear he meant what he said. The meaning was conveyed in the way it was expressed, radiating out of him in tight, simmering threats. In a moment, I could see everyone in his place, repeating the same words: the onlookers, my teachers, my neighbors, our elders. *Was he the messenger?* I thought about the "halves" I represented and pictured my parents and their beautiful faces. My dad had sandy brown hair, fair skin, green eyes, and a striking jaw line. I pictured him singing and dancing with my mother. My mom had milky smooth skin and dark, wavy hair that framed her gorgeous face. She had almond eyes, high cheekbones, a button nose, full lips, and a little gap between her two front teeth. She stood gracefully and in moments of excitement she would bounce around in place and give two thumbs-up with a big laugh. She would often join my father in a waltz as they hummed a tune—that is, before Mom eventually stepped on Dad's foot.

Perhaps, from the point of view of our neighbors, it felt unfair that an interracial couple could be so liberated—achieving happiness and advancing in their wealth and opportunities, all the while being in a loving, equitable relationship. I wonder if the spite I heard in that boy's words was envy. As a five-year-old mixed-race girl, half in and half out, I became the ideal, accessible target. In retrospect, I should have asked him, "Which half are you referring to?" I should have held up a mirror so he might see his own reflection.

My bilingual gifts led me into rooms filled with misfit kids— all boys.

When I got home that day after school, I didn't tell my parents about the bus-stop incident. It would have been a perfect opportunity for my mom to tell me not to let the bastards get me down—her encouraging, go-to phrase for moments like these. Instead, I walked into the bathroom and stared at my face. *What did I see?* Nothing out of the ordinary: the same face staring back. I made goofy faces, serious faces, sad faces. I pushed the encounter aside. Being half my parents was special and looking back at the reflection of their mixing gave me pride.

A YEAR LATER, my parents shared that I was going to have a baby brother. I was so excited about the news. It felt like a gift from them. They were *giving* me a brother. I blurted out, "Now I won't be alone when you die!" with a big, pleased smile on my face. My parents looked at each other, surprised by my comment, but agreed with its practicality. In hindsight, what I probably meant was that with a brother, I wouldn't be alone. There'd be another hapa in the family with whom I could share collective experiences, which was not something I could do with anyone else in my life. Jon and I could compare notes on how people reacted to us and how to navigate the world. With him in my life, there was reassurance, safety, and connection.

My brother took his time arriving in the world. He enjoyed Ma's favorite foods well past his due date. Enjoying the comfort and warmth of her belly, Jon decided to join our family on the summer solstice of 1986. Even though he weighed nine pounds and six ounces, he and Ma had an easier, quicker birth experience. He came out the exact gender as expected and was quiet, observant, and curious about the new world around him. Ma ended up feeding him the popular 1980s baby formula, part of which he often threw up with a cute grin on his face. During those early days, the house smelled of spoiled milk. When Jon began to walk, he'd enter my room as I was playing with my My Little Ponies with a big smile and drool down his face, holding a bottle of formula upside down, droplets dripping on the floor as he torpedoed my ponies with his monster baby feet. He was the Godzilla to my toys, and we'd play chase to avoid further destruction.

I loved engaging with my little brother—who looked like me—in a world full of imagination, play, and adventure. I pretended to be a horse, galloping on all fours and jumping over objects, and he would observe. We'd rip up magazines, share snacks, and when I'd push something too far in our imaginative game, he'd angrily shout, "Tupid Ing!" I couldn't help but smile given how he still hadn't mastered the "s" in most words. It reminded me of phrases I'd come up with at home, like "All right all body, see you too-morning" and my name for windshield wipers, "whimper shy-pers." Jon's mastery of the "s" sound would come later, but at the time, I loved the imperfect words we made up, that we had a secret, shared understanding of their meaning.

When Ma was out on business trips, Jon and I would play "fashion show" in her walk-in closet. Ma's wardrobe had all kinds of textures—furs, feathers, sparkles, and sequins that shined. We would look up in awe at the bursts of colors and graze our hands along the different fabrics.

Our attention was diverted towards the lineup of heels, all neatly arranged at the more reachable floor level, with such a range in height and design. We would take turns sticking our feet into the base of a chosen pair and shuffle-walk the runway from the closet entrance to the end of the bedroom, strike a pose, and return for the finale—kicking off each heel to the back of Mom's cavernous closet. We were mini fashionistas, just like Ma. We'd burst with laughter before finding another pair to walk the runway in. We felt Ma's joy through those heels.

Ma had a pair of silver heels that I savored. Each time I wore them I imagined how she felt walking in them—confident and in her essence, all eyes on her. I admired my mother. She was expressive and routinely experimenting with new hairstyles and fashion trends. When she got ready for a cocktail party, she'd put on a metallic '80s dress, those silver heels, and makeup. She looked drop-dead gorgeous, and I pictured her as the life of the party, which Ba always confirmed when they returned home. Ma was comfortable in her skin; she was unfailingly kind to people and brought out depth in those around her.

Ma never seemed to come home upset or angry about the state of her closet floor. I don't know if Ba snuck in and put all the heels neatly back in place, or if she saw the mess we left post-fashion show and chuckled at the fun we must have had. Ma could be demanding, asking about our grades and requesting that I play her the latest piece I learned on the piano. She wanted both her children to be obedient, dutiful, well-behaved kids who honored their mom and dad—proof that we were a happy household. When we fit that mold, she was pleased. When she returned home from work trips in Europe, she was often in a high mood; she'd unfold subway maps on the kitchen table and show us where she journeyed and how she got around. Ma regaled us with stories of her whiskey-sour evenings among her all-male cast of colleagues. She was fierce and feisty, dedicated to her team, her ambition, and the adventure of exploring each city she traveled to.

But I sometimes found her crying in bed, in contrast to her naturally confident, leader self. Sometimes it was because of us, but I often felt it was due to the weight of the discrimination she experienced because of the glass-and-bamboo ceiling. Time and time again, a man would be hired between her and her boss, removing the opportunity for her own career advancement. She even attended a program at Smith College that prepared women in tech for executive leadership. Despite her efforts and her visionary, pioneering approach, she was passed over again and again. Yet she stuck to the perspective that "in order to make real change, you need to start in the belly of the beast." And for her, that meant making change from within the corporate world.

Every now and then, I'd sit on the staircase listening to her re-recording her voicemail greeting because she didn't like the way her accent sounded. She'd trip up on a word, pause, and then re-record. She'd play it back. Delete it and start over. This would go on for an hour. Pausing. Sighing. Starting from the top. The amount of time she spent crafting this message was painful to listen to—it was time stolen from her joy, her weekend, her rest and recovery. I doubted any of her co-workers ever gave this much thought and attention to their voicemail greetings. It was as though her accent held a truth that put her in a category of *other*. I knew what that felt like.

One day as I was listening to her on the stairs, I decided to act. I walked around the corner and faced her. "Ma, you sound great! Don't worry about what anyone thinks!" I said encouragingly. I was about to add, "Don't let those bastards get you down," but I saw surprise ignite her face and anger push me away.

"Leave me alone," she hissed in defense of her exposed shame.

I paused before taking off, wishing she would take me in her arms for loving and seeing her. I thought she might hug me and agree, leave the voicemail behind and suggest we do something together like get chocolate and vanilla swirl cones—our favorite treat to get together. I wished that I had reminded her of her uniqueness and power, her bravery in leading this life across such distinct cultures, her tenacity in embracing days filled with challenge, even disappointment. I wanted her to know that she wasn't alone. She had us, and to us she was everything.

Ma didn't divulge her struggles as an immigrant. She seemed to keep them at bay, a secret that only she could carry. I can't imagine how challenging it was for her to learn an entirely new language and culture, let alone be a tech pioneer and a young mother of two hapa kids. One of her journal entries offers a glimpse into her experience:

Some of the most dramatic and permanent changes occurred in my life during the ten short years from age sixteen to twenty-six. The most challenging was coming to the US to study at age nineteen. My life up to that point was like canoeing in a beautiful green river on a sunny day where the water was calm and serene. I could see my reflection as I leaned out of the boat. The scenery was gorgeous: I could hear the singing of birds and smell the sweet fragrance of the honeysuckle. The river carried me peacefully downstream.

Then it turned and narrowed, and the narrowing of the rock banks created a turbulent current. Without warning I was propelled into the white rapids. Suddenly I was gasping for air and struggling to keep my head above the churning water. Panic gripped me and I thought, Oh, Lord, I'm drowning! Help! Somebody please help me!

MA GASPED FOR AIR during difficult times throughout her career. I watched as she showed signs of pain and brokenness and searched for nurturing and healing. Church became a way for her to seek salvation, but this drove a wedge between us. Neither my brother nor I liked being forced to go to church. It was part of Ma's requirement that we be dutiful children. She was hell-bent on being immersed as a member, even a leader, of a Christian community, and an Asian one at that.

If we didn't want to go to church, she would dig her heels in and guilt-trip us into going. Church was *every* Sunday. It was as if church gave her a reprieve, hope. It was where she felt seen and heard. Dad followed and supported her, and they even ran the youth group for a while. I hope she felt comfort and reassurance connecting with fellow Asian community members navigating the clash with, and often a brutal onboarding to, American culture. Yet that's not always what the church offered. Instead, the community navigated similar issues around who belonged and who didn't. And our interracial family was often a target.

"Hunxue'er" (混血兒) is a Chinese term used to refer to people of mixed race. It literally means "mixed-blood child" and is used to describe all mixed-race people. On the one hand, our mixed features are idealized by many in the Asian community. But, on the other hand, we're also a reminder of white barbarians infiltrating Taiwanese society. As a mixed-blood child at an Asian church, I didn't feel seen, respected, loved, or safe.

As a kid, the two things I mildly enjoyed about church were singing and harmonizing at the beginning of the sermon, and the open lunch buffet after the service, which was filled with heaps of noodles, rice, and stir-fried dishes. But seeing Ma sing next to me with her arm raised to touch the Holy Spirit made me feel like perhaps she might be a witch after all.

At the age of ten, while Ma was at a women's group meeting possibly speaking in tongues, I sat near the church stage looking at the instruments played earlier that morning, waiting to go home. I was by myself until the door opened and a pack of teens entered for their youth group meeting, which was conducted across a few church pews. One of the boys looked at me. As I started to leave, the boy murmured in disdain, "Half piece of shit."

I paused, blindsided. Did this Asian brother just call me that? I was hurt and angry. I looked at him with cutting eyes, a familiar question rising within me: *Which half are you referring to?* I glared at him. *Take a long look at your own refection in the mirror.*

If Ma was exhausted by the patriarchy in corporate America, I was exhausted by it in church.

I argued with her about how she prioritized her faith above her own family. I wondered, looking at the sea of wanting faces in the congregation, if everyone was in search of something they needed, longed for, or even craved. If I had a prayer, it was for inclusion and belonging. It was for justice and liberation. It was for kindness and acceptance.

OUTSIDE OF CHURCH, growing up, I was asked one of two questions on a daily basis by random strangers: "What are you?" and "Where are you / your people from?" These questions were invasive, tiring, repetitive. Why didn't anyone ask me the real question they wanted to know, that is, "What is your ethnic background?" I began to study and draw my face. I'd stare into my eyes, looking into my soul. *Who am I? What do I see? Do I see* me *in there?*

Despite how normal this line of questioning had become, I was always caught off guard. I had to consider my options. Would I be cheeky, spiteful, honest, devoid of emotion, full of emotion, angry, withdrawn, even defeated? If I responded with "I'm human" or "I'm a girl," they'd get annoyed, even heated. Which always led to them digging in their heels and switching to the second-most popular question, "Where are you from?" To which I would respond, "New Jersey."

They'd get frustrated and impatient, as if I were stupid and didn't understand the question. They'd ask, "No, where are *your* people from?" And if I answered, "The United States of America. The planet Earth," anger stepped

It always felt invasive.

It always felt rude.

It always felt like

they were crossing

a boundary.

in front of embarrassment. They—almost always white people—wanted and demanded to know the answer. They felt they had the authority, the right to know.

It always felt invasive.

It always felt rude.

It always felt like they were crossing a boundary.

If Ba was nearby, they'd address him and ask inappropriately, "Were you in the service?" I'd watch my dad maneuver around this offensive question. He was a people pleaser but had a family to protect. Perhaps the most unsettling version of this exchange was when a stranger, staring at my dad and me at a local garage sale when I was still a teenager, bluntly asked him, "Is that your girlfriend?" *Ugh, what the hell is wrong with you? Ewwwww.*

"This is my daughter," Ba said. Eyes rolled where I wanted heads in their place.

I watched Ba de-escalate and choose not to engage in anger. He let these battles go, even if they hurt and upset him. Eventually, his frustration was expressed at home in fights or in occasionally throwing and breaking things, hitting the dashboard of the car, even driving away for hours. Sometimes, I'd wait by the window and wonder if the other half of my parental unit would return. It was unsettling how much the outside world could impact our inner world at home. I was left in limbo to wonder at the display of unrequited social and cultural acceptance.

This spotlight on my appearance and race was othering; it was an unwanted interruption in my daily life. It was a constant reminder that I didn't belong, that I was the one who stood out. I'd dread filling out those surveys in school about what race you were. I was confused by the minimal options staring back at me: white, black, Asian, Hispanic, OTHER. That word, in bold as if proclaiming its stronghold on my identity, was my only option. I am other, and a spotlight always followed. For a kid, it didn't make sense. Why all the fuss? Why did they need to know *so badly*?

As early as first grade, I used to place orders at the seafood counter at ShopRite for whole red snapper with "the head still on, cleaned and descaled." I simply restated instructions from Ma, who would rather delegate this awkward order to her daughter who "spoke good English." It saved her from repeating herself and feeling self-conscious about her accent, which drew its own kind of unwanted attention.

Most people ordered fish fillets. If they ever ordered a whole fish, it was always with the head chopped off. I was direct and clear. After a while, I noticed the regular butcher gave me a look of dismay when I'd place this order. I couldn't tell if the look was good or bad, half good or half bad. I took the fish and marched to the checkout counter, hoping one of my parents would let me go next door to the local toy store where I could feast my eyes on the My Little Pony aisle and avoid the "What are you?" questions from adults.

At home, Ma steamed the whole red snapper with sliced ginger, scallions, Szechuan spices, bok choy, and jalapeños. It was delicious, light, warming, and soothing. I'd play piano for her afterwards. She'd write in her journal while cozied up on a loveseat, listening to me play as she wrote. She would hum and, at times, close her eyes when I looked towards her. I savored these moments as time to just be with my mom and connect with her nonverbally. Be in her presence, next to her thoughts, and one with our imaginations. A harmony.

In my absence, Ma would listen to music on her single-CD player set up in her makeshift sanctuary. She wrote often, interpreting her dreams wrapped in spiritual meaning, using a mix of Chinese characters and English words. As a child, I would carry my imagination to and from my room and to our backyard. While Ma found an outlet just for herself, I wondered where to locate mine. I was an expressive kid, full of confidence and a sense of self and self-worth. These interactions with adults were limiting and repetitive. Hearing the same tune, you want to change the channel, but I couldn't find the dial in my interactions with public life. I wanted to connect with others deeply, I felt that inclination, but I had to turn inward to protect myself from the constant inquisition—the spotlight I could not escape.

That is, until one day when my world serendipitously changed. Playing outside in the backyard and taking a break from the piano and the world of adults, I heard an unfamiliar sound coming from behind the woods that bordered our house. Loud, strong, new. Powerful. I listened as the sound got closer and steadier. It was riveting! Thump, thump thump, thump, thump thump. My heartbeat was strong, unafraid—I felt ignited with every beat of this thrilling sound. As if a calling, an awakening, a liberation was upon me. I was transfixed.

Through the trees, I saw three riders on horseback—a mix of big muscles and hooves, leather tack, iron stirrups, and riding boots. *Equestrians!* As they passed by, I followed as if I had signed up for their cause. I ran through the brush and got whacked by tree branches as I passed by neighbors' homes and backyards I had never crossed before. Ba had come out to see where I went and followed close by. I made it my job not to lose track of these women on horseback. I would have kept following them forever.

Just like when I walked oblivious and carefree through a sea of stares at the airport as a toddler, I knew this was where I belonged. I belonged wherever these horses and riders were going, and nothing was going to stop me from getting there.

Mommy with her nice, nice baby in the backyard of our first home.

top Ma and I sharing a soda.

bottom Jon joins our family so I won't die alone.

三

EQUESTRIAN BARN RAT

THE FIRST HORSE I ever rode was an old palomino named Sally. I was five years old, just about to turn six. I was so small they had to wrap the leather stirrups multiple times so that my little-kid legs would fit over her spine, with the irons resting at the flap of the saddle. There's a faded picture of this moment Ba captured, which I still have. I'm holding the reins proudly with a huge grin, showcasing a few missing teeth and wearing that purple puffy jacket from the bus stop with a pair of rain boots. I didn't yet have riding gear.

In the photo, I'm radiating joy. It felt so natural to be on top of a horse. Ba often shares his experience from that first day. Once the instructor got me situated, she told me to wait while she got other riders mounted. As she walked away, I gave the horse a nudging kick and off we went into the ring. My concerned father shouted, "Ingrid, Ingrid, INGRID!" as the horse marched forward, neither of us looking back.

Who would have known that just a fifteen-minute drive from our home, off Woods Road, was Phoenix Farms, a small oasis of an equestrian facility hidden in central New Jersey. I loved leaving the residential homes behind and turning down that long, winding gravel driveway. A dreamy equestrian world would appear: two stables, four paddocks, and two barns. Phoenix Farms became the epicenter of my young life. Shortly after that first day, I became a full-blown horse girl: everything I did was connected to horses, on and off the farm.

At home, I advanced from galloping on all fours to setting up entire courses around the basement to jump over. I emulated horse behaviors. I even ate like a horse—who doesn't love apples, carrots, and oats? I was enamored by their strength, beauty, power, and size. They symbolized independence. It was a gift to be around horses and an even greater gift to ride them.

My parents were willing and able to pay for riding lessons, but, in a few short years, my riding advanced. In order to lessen the cost of riding as frequently as I wished to, I was given the option of working at the stable. So, starting at the age of nine, each summer I worked from 6 a.m. to 6 p.m. and rode three horses throughout the day. Soon, I was able to pick up fifty-pound bags of feed and stack multiple bales of hay on a large, rickety wheelbarrow I'd maneuver between barns. I cleaned copious amounts of tack, washed multiple loads of horse blankets, and air-dried saddle cushions. I mucked endless clumps of horse manure and urine-soaked shavings in stalls, filling bucket after bucket and dumping them in the field spreader. I scrubbed water buckets and groomed horses, taking them to and from paddocks. I ended each day by sweeping the entire stable, top to bottom.

I wasn't the only horse-obsessed "barn rat"—a term for the girls who showed up every day at the stable to work for the opportunity to ride. There was a handful of us, each devoted to and focused on horses. Every morning, we'd review the whiteboard of chores and find our names assigned. Off we'd go to complete each morning task, take a break to ride, eat our packed lunches, ride again, then work some more. Every now and then the trainers would order sandwiches, and we'd all eat together. Being around strong women inspired me.

My trainers were twenty-something women who took equestrian living very seriously. They were mentors who were brave in the saddle and showed us how to fix a bad habit when a horse needed discipline—and how to know when a horse needed a break and time in pasture. We were taught to use crops to encourage movement and dissuade bad behavior; we were trained to communicate with horses by using our reins and our legs to increase or decrease a horse's gait. Every movement had a purpose and a signal.

For general riding lessons, the stable had a mix of school horses that were either donated or in semi-retirement. There were also elite, more expensive horses owned by dressage and hunt seat equitation riders. These riders ranged in age from their early twenties to their late seventies. The trainers and stable owner had their own horses, which they rode daily. As barn rats, we rode a mix of the school horses to retrain them as needed. And every now and then, we'd get to ride a horse that needed exercising but whose owner couldn't make it to the stable.

Each horse had their name engraved on a plate in front of their stall. I knew each of them as if we were all part of a common herd. I greeted each horse in the morning and said my goodbyes before I walked to the blue Volvo when Ba arrived to take me home. I would return home filthy. Ma required me to shed and toss my soiled clothes into the washing machine before entering the house and heading to the shower. I remember how it felt to turn on warm water on my tired muscles and clean off the dirt in my hair, on my skin, and under my fingernails. Afterwards, I'd join my family seated at the dining table for dinner. I'd be famished, eating like a horse deep in her rice bucket.

MA RARELY ENTERED my horse world. As I ran towards all things horses, she stayed far away from the dirt, dust, and danger that the stable symbolized. Maybe it was hard to watch me go over jumps and see the risk of harm at each turn. Although Ma rarely, if ever, showed up to lessons or horse shows, she supported my passion. She never made me feel weird for thinking I was a horse or that I could communicate with horses. She just didn't want the barn-rat part of me in her clean home.

Over the next five years, I gained more proficiency and skill as an equestrian. My parents leased a pony named Ticket to Ride and then bought a dapple-gray quarter horse named Ziggy that I called Silver Lining for the show ring. We owned Ziggy only for two years as he was tough for a young kid like me to train, but he joined the other school horses after our dedicated time together. Then, in my early teen years, I co-leased a beautiful brown thoroughbred named Mason, followed by a white mare named Layla. Between those horses, I trained and entered the show ring with Lloyd, Blackie, Ricky, and several others.

Horses were my everything, and that everything came with a hefty price tag. The combination of fees for food, veterinarians, farriers, horse-show travel and entry, additional training sessions, and boarding was expensive. I remember as a ten-year-old looking at the handwritten invoices, each line item adding up to a big dollar amount for the 1990s: $550. Owning or leasing a horse was a major commitment of time, money, and training. It required dedication and funding.

Ma and Ba wrote the checks. At dinner each day, they listened to my stories about my day at the barn. Ma would remind me to be careful. She and Ba saw my work ethic forming. Where other kids consumed pop culture and MTV, I was absorbed by a passion that took great effort, trust, and care.

More of my weekends began including horse shows. Ba would drive me to the barn at 3 a.m. so I could braid and prep the horse I would ride. He'd drop me off and a while later bring back a dozen donuts from Dunkin' while I buffed up my riding gear and made sure I had my entire show-ring outfit ready.

At one horse show, Ma surprised us and showed up with Jon in tow. It was when we owned Ziggy, who got set off easily and would spook in the ring. Ma had listened to my stories of my training woes. She knew I had faith, patience, and determination with Ziggy's training, but there was little improvement. Even more surprising was that Ma came to the horse trailer, a compact, kinetic place that she had never stepped into before. Now she walked right up to Ziggy and petted his nose and face. "Don't be afraid, you can do it," she cooed. It might not have been my face she touched to calm and soothe, but I was moved by her efforts on my behalf.

She joined Ba and Jon in the stands. As I entered the ring, Ziggy started to spook, but I looked over at my family and felt their support. I gave Ziggy a reassuring pet and calmed my anxious mind. I let go of trying to control him or the outcome. And Ziggy had his best performance that round and we actually won! As I accepted the blue ribbon, I looked over and saw Ma smiling and cheering in the stands. I beamed ear to ear. She was actually proud of me.

DURING THESE PIVOTAL YEARS from childhood to adolescence, I learned how to build trust with horses and communicate both verbally and nonverbally—and, most importantly, how to handle fear and unpredictability by centering myself and calming my breath. I mentally and physically found an internal rhythm I encouraged each horse I rode to align with. I picked up on their moods and emotions, their behaviors, and their moments of joy. They understood me in a way I felt no human could. We were a team.

During these years, I did well in most hunt seat equitation and jumper competitions, and I built up experience across the multiple horses I showed. In the ring, full of risk and possibility, it was just me, the horse, and the course ahead of us. I had to memorize the different combinations of jumps and follow the prescribed routine. But it didn't always go well.

Once, a horse I loved named Lloyd panicked in the ring and refused every jump. I was shocked because he was behaving radically different from our training sessions. After every refusal and bolt, we'd circle back until he eventually went over the jump. I calmly encouraged him to finish the entire course. It took a long time to finish, and we were both exhausted. Each time we got to a jump, I hung on for dear life, not knowing if he'd refuse or finally launch over it. He reacted and behaved as if I'd beat him after each refusal. I never did.

I later learned that an experience in his past led to these behaviors, causing his demotion from a champion to a donated school horse. As I left the ring, the audience applauded. They had been on the edge of their seats watching the drama of Lloyd's reactions, anxious to see how we would get through the course unscathed. The irony is that at the start of the competition, Lloyd and I won the flat, non-jumping round, the best out of fifty riders. I held on to that blue ribbon. Because during our jumper competition, I won his trust and partnership. I didn't give up on him, nor did I give up on myself. I had given up the competition—it was more important to show Lloyd we could get through the experience together. In making that choice, I learned what kind of leader I would be. Maybe Ma knew all along that riding would provide important lessons to her daughter.

I felt camaraderie with horses. They gave me a window into their stories and their lives. I so wished I could understand their language, verbally ask them questions, and listen to their answers. One horse I grew to love, named Blackie, expressed himself in the most profound way. In fact, he taught me about psychological safety, the emotional and physical toll of trauma, and how abuse can keep you caged.

Blackie was stunning. He was a huge Dutch Warmblood with a smooth and powerful gait. When we were in the ring, it felt like we flew. But in his stall, which is meant to be a horse's safe space and home, he was totally different. For Blackie, his home was where he had been whipped and beaten by a rider at his former stable. The stable owner at Phoenix Farms explained his past as she demonstrated how to safely enter his stall, given how angry and defensive he would react. He pinned his ears back and snapped at anyone who walked by. He'd kick at the baseboards and snarl, dragging his teeth along the stall rails. He tirelessly protected his stall, warning no one to enter. And when you needed to, you were scared. You could never enter his stall wearing riding gear. You had to enter cautiously and back towards him so he wouldn't attack you. Only then could you slip on his halter and a lead line to calmly walk him out. Blackie had bitten several people and routinely lunged at visitors who walked past his stall.

And yet, once out of his stall, he'd pause and let out an exhausted exhale. It was as if he was so tired of having to protect himself and deflect potential danger. He turned into a magnificent version of himself that I loved, reminding me of the horse in the book *Black Beauty*. I wished I could have spoken with him as, say, an adult therapist would, helping him heal and let go of the past, to live more in the present. But neither of us had those skills. All the love and reassurance he received outside of his stall had no bearing once he was back inside of it. He would transition immediately—ears pinned back, teeth chomping at the bars. Every day, the last stall I passed was Blackie's. I knew that saying goodbye or giving him a carrot was pointless. In his stall, he was in a vortex where I could no longer reach him. All his fear and pain masked with anger and self-preservation.

IRONICALLY, I, TOO, would experience my own stall incident. It happened in the upper barn on a spring afternoon when I was about ten years old. It was a typical day. I had reviewed the whiteboard of chores and saw which horses needed riding and training. Part of the day's work included chores in the upper little barn. To get to the little barn, you had to walk up a dirt road, just past where the owner lived. Behind her home was a small barn of about six stalls, three on each side. Down a short hall was an entrance to the entire paddock, which wrapped around the little barn. We barn rats didn't frequent the little barn given that most of the work we were required to do was in the main barn. But every now and then, the chore list sent us up there.

Today it was my turn. I was to bring several bales of hay to the little barn. It was already getting warm, and the hay I had loaded onto a large wood-and-steel cart kept the heat close to my breath as I pushed up the hill between the barns. Given there was a slight incline, it required effort. I had to pace myself or sprint and drop the cart for a much-needed break. I focused on the task and eventually arrived at the little barn sweating and panting.

What surprised me was that the other, slightly older barn rats were up at the little barn, too. I wasn't really paying attention to their tasks and continued loading the hay into the storage area. I picked up a mucking rake to clean out one of the stalls. The first stall was empty as the horse had been brought out to the paddock to stretch its legs and wander. The stable door was wide open, retracted into the wall as these doors were designed. I began mucking the stall and had my back to the door when I heard it: the heavy door rolling against the upper steel, closing abruptly, and the steel lock moving into place. Confused, I turned around and saw three barn rats' faces against the steel bars, as if they were looking in at the zoo animal they had just caught. The older girl laughed. A fourth girl came over holding a hose. I placed the muck rake to the side and kept my eyes on them as I stood at the back of the stall. The girl holding the hose had a strange look on her face—and she was smiling. *Why am I locked in the stall?*

The next thing I knew, I felt it—the blast of cold water darting onto my body from the jet setting on the hose. I tried bracing myself against it while I leaned into the back stall wall. The hose was aimed at my torso, spraying up towards my face. I remember closing my eyes, quietly holding my breath, and turning sideways, lifting one of my hands into my chest like a hoof. I turned into a horse. I turned into Blackie.

After several minutes, while I remained quiet and kept my eyes closed, the water stopped. I was soaked. I slowly opened my eyes and glanced over at the stall doors. One of the more empathetic girls opened the stall and let me out as the pack leader laughed. She had a pleased look on her face, like she enjoyed completing an act of harm. I didn't know what a bully was until that moment.

I wasn't sure why she attacked me. She was the owner's favorite. They looked alike, were both blonde, and had nicknames for one another. It seemed that she always got to ride her favorite horse. One time when I was scheduled to go to a horse show, I was switched out last minute so she could go. My dad, confused about that decision, asked the owner about the change. She said that she needed to give other girls a fair amount of ring time.

I started to feel like I was the "other" in this horse world. I was always talking to horses, and was often mocked. Although everyone at the barn shared a love of horses, not everyone wanted to *be* a horse or thought they could speak with them. I'd soon get locked in yet another stall as a gag to prove that the horse I was talking to didn't care and wouldn't talk back to me. This time, I silently cried, realizing that part of this was true. The horse couldn't help me or talk to me; it was curious about my presence and eventually nudged me before eating its hay as the gag wrapped up. Maybe I wasn't a horse after all.

Almost thirty years later, I would finally share these experiences with my parents. I don't know how I went home and shut them out, as their impact burrowed deep into my psyche, channeling bits of insecurity, inferiority, judgement, and anger within me. My warrior spirit had to combat these new feelings and thoughts. Messages replayed in my head about how misunderstood and disliked I was.

One day, as I was closing the stable, I passed by Blackie's stall. I saw his ears pinned back. He was barring his teeth at the bars and I almost wept. Deep down inside I made a promise with myself. If Blackie couldn't find his path to healing and peace, I would do it for both our sakes.

MA CONTINUED to maintain her distance from my horsey world, but one day she told me a story that changed me forever. It was a story about my great-grandmother Shi Qing (1900–1981) in China whose surname was Hu. She was fierce and had actually fought in the Second Sino-Japanese War. She unbound her feet, which were by then disfigured, and rode horses while shooting at the enemy, guns in both hands. Ma told me that I got my horseback riding mastery from her. It was as if Ma was telling me that I was part of a special herd of women—a strong lineage. Listening to her story, I felt a deep connection to my strength, determination, and spirit.

In the early days of the Second Sino-Japanese War, Shi Qing served as the principal of the No. 3 Primary School in Kaifeng, the provincial capital of Henan. On the eve of Kaifeng's fall at the hands of the Imperial Japanese Army, she led more than 120 young women to battle. Many women sacrificed their lives. After surviving, Shi Qing traveled along the Longhai Railway to Lanzhou, Gansu Province, and saw displaced children along the way. While in Lanzhou, she took in more than 1,200 children and established the Northwest Salesian Home in 1939.

A graduate of Yanjing University, Shi Qing went on to found Yi Kuang orphanage and a handful of kindergarten schools in Taiwan. I researched female figures from this period who might have been tied to my great-grandmother. I read about the Red Detachment, the first all-women

Listening to Ma's story,
I learned I was part of
a special herd—a strong
lineage. I felt a deep
connection to my strength,
determination, and spirit.

military brigade in 1930s China. And before the Red Detachment, there was Qiu Jin (1875–1907), "the Chinese Joan of Arc," who is said to have "challenged gender roles and demanded equal rights and opportunities for women." She is seen as a heroine who also fought for revolution, even though that led to her execution.

I pictured my great-grandma in the moment she decided to unbind her feet, how she went against what people wanted of her and expected her to be. Going against the norm, she educated herself in how best to defend her community and country. At that time, during China's Qing dynasty, female children of high-class families had their feet bound—basically crippling them—to demonstrate their privileged status and that they did not have to work. Foot binding was also eroticized, which is a whole other aspect of that trend. I think about young women growing up without the use of their feet, how captive they must have felt. You could not run towards freedom. As an equestrian, freedom is the wind on your face as you ride a horse; it's the coexistence of you and an animal galloping forward. I wondered if my great-grandma felt that the first time she got on horseback after saving her poor feet. I hope to discover more of her story in my lifetime.

Listening to Ma telling me this story for the first time, pointing her fingers like guns as she described my great-grandmother shooting the enemy while on horseback, I felt connected to my ancestral lineage. Across time and geography, identity and circumstance, we were connected, even by our love of horses. I was part of a bigger story taking shape. As this sank in, Ma watched my expression, holding the moment and its impact. She looked at me and said, "We are warrior spirits." I believed her. She was a fighter with a broken, martyred side. What an overwhelming experience it must have been for her to be both at once.

AS THE YEARS went by, I continued riding and cleaning out stalls. I even made friends with some of the other barn rats. I was blooming into a strong rider and a young woman. My features were less goofy, and I was maturing. I received compliments on my riding skills, which were accompanied by comments on how I had the right *body type* for equitation. I was doing well in the show ring and my relationship with my female trainers evolved. Many opened up about experiences from their teen years, which revealed a softer side to them that I rarely saw in the ring. I knew that they cared for me and that each had a younger self who had once been just as horse-obsessed as me.

I was around thirteen when the opportunity to move to Italy and train more seriously was brought up by my new trainer. I had mixed feelings about it. It was dawning on me that my *performance* as a rider was becoming more valued than anything else. I felt like I was being pulled further away from what gave me the most joy in riding: just me and the horse, cantering in a field with the wind whipping at my face. Freedom and independence.

Training was strenuous. One day after a session, I decided that instead of cooling down and walking the horse out in the field, I'd take the horse out on a short trail ride. It was a mini rebellion that expressed my need to reconnect with what made me love riding in the first place—adventure.

What was meant to be a short ride turned into an extended jaunt through the forest and into farming fields, walking the perimeter of other properties. And then, in the distance, I saw the back of a series of track homes and knew exactly where I was.

We walked along the path of trees that divided the neighborhood from the field and slowly passed by the house I grew up in—by my teen years we had moved to another, newer development. I thought about my little five-year-old self, running to meet the sounds I was now making as an equestrian eight years later. I found the path that I had once run to, where my dad had followed, where it all began.

I knew riding in the development was not allowed. But I persisted. I led the horse onto the path and headed towards that old bus stop where that popular fifth grader had called me a half piece of shit. The irony is that when we got to the intersection, the horse paused, lifted its tail, and laid a hot steamy one onto the asphalt. I laughed out loud and smiled widely. *Here's a whole piece, an entire pile of shit, y'all.*

I continued past the bus stop. I didn't feel like turning back. We headed towards the pond where I went fishing with my dad under the willow tree. I picked up a canter just as a teenaged boy riding his bike waved and came to join the scene. We expressed a mutual respect, him riding his bike, me riding my horse. He headed his way, turning back one last time. It was a scene that might never happen again: a young, mixed-race woman cantering her way across a white neighborhood on a liberated beast.

It was already getting dark by the time I got back to the barn. The owner was waiting for me, exasperated, worried about where I'd been and if I was alright. She expressed disappointment and frustration. Had she asked me, I would have told her how incredible and glorious the experience had been. How I preferred this kind of pleasure riding. But I knew she didn't want to hear that from me. And so, I bathed the horse, cleaned my tack, and followed all the routines of wrapping up. Before turning out the lights and closing the barn doors, I glanced at Blackie. He looked at me with curiosity, uncertain about my departure. As if he knew that this was all coming to an end. As if the days of seeing me pass by his stall might soon be over.

THE SUMMER BEFORE high school, I had the opportunity to try out for sport teams before the term began. Despite having never played field hockey, I got a varsity position on the team. Only two freshmen were chosen. I was excited about playing a new sport. I wanted to know what it was like to be a team member, especially with other women. Varsity required yet another extensive training schedule and for a while, I tried balancing both field hockey and equestrian training. Until, one day, that balance tipped.

I arrived at the barn late and physically exhausted. My trainer was annoyed by my tardiness. She had planned a complex set of field jumps that day and I was to ride Bart, a massive Clydesdale and Dutch Warmblood horse, the tallest at the barn. As I groomed over Bart's massive muscles, I could feel my own aching and shaking. Plus, I was hungry.

An hour later, I was covered in two layers of sweat. One that had long dried, from field hockey, and a new layer from the rigorous equestrian training. Bart had a ring of foam around his mouth. On any other day, keeping his strong gait collected was manageable. But today it was challenging.

The natural strides of his canter were gigantic. Where other horses took four strides between consecutive jumps, he could do it in two. You had to collect his force and use that to leap over jumps and execute hairpin turns to get to the next set of jumps.

I was almost finished with the course. Rounding a corner, I had my eyes on the final jump: it contained six vertical, parallel bars with brushes sticking out between them. To the right, both Bart and I could see the barn. I think he could feel my hunger, which made him feel compelled to get back in his stall to eat. He was antsy. I tightened my reins. All I had to do was keep him steady and go over this final jump. I pictured the thumping of his massive hooves echoing the thumping of my overworked heart. I counted the strides to the final jump. Four, three, two, one... and then, darkness.

I remember coming to rather quickly. I had somersaulted off Bart onto the ground, one of my rare falls. Bart had cantered straight through the jump. I had missed signaling to jump, and so, he didn't. I looked around for him. He was nearby, happily eating grass, an appetizer to the dinner that awaited him. The trainer hovered over me. I expected her to check that I hadn't broken anything. I pictured her kneeling down and asking me, "Ingrid, are you alright?" and then helping me back up. Instead, her tone was of anger and blame: "You could have broken his leg." She turned around, started walking to the horse to collect his reins, and said, "Get up and do it again."

After you fall off a horse, it's generally good practice to get back on. But this time I couldn't, I wouldn't. I had always listened to, obeyed, and aimed to please my trainers. This was the first time I said no. I walked right to Bart, checked his legs, and looked into his eyes. I knew he didn't want to continue. I watched his relief when I took the reins over his head and walked him back towards the stable. I wouldn't do the course over. I had been trained to ride a certain way—it was ingrained in me and was no longer bringing me joy. I had to listen to the animal I loved the most who seemed to be saying, *Go live your life, kid. We will be here when you're ready to come ride again.*

As I packed up my gear, I knew that I wouldn't be going to Italy. And that I would no longer continue working with this trainer, nor would I continue with this kind of training. I had become so immersed in the world of horses that I had avoided diving into the deep end of adolescence. I was curious about boys, I was into fashion and makeup, and I wanted to experience life on my terms, as a full-blown teenager. Not solely as a performer. Which riding had become more about.

As I left the barn that day, I knew that this episode of my life was wrapping up. I called each horse by name, touched their noses wedged between the stall bars, and felt gratitude for all they had taught me. I looked at them one more time as steam rose from their nostrils, highlighted by the setting sun. "I'll be back," I said. I was no longer a barn rat. But a horse girl I'd be in my heart, forever.

WHEN I ENTERED freshman year of high school, grunge was in fashion. I fully embraced the style by wearing Doc Martens, a flannel shirt and jeans, and eye makeup and lipstick. I parted my long, wavy dark hair in the middle. I was

As a young woman who looked different—*exotic*—a new kind of unshakeable target had been placed upon me.

lean and strong, tan from working all summer in the sun, and I looked much older than fourteen. Walking down the high school's hallway was like walking out of my mother's closet.

Boys noticed me right away, girls gravitated towards becoming friends. I quickly caught on and learned how to French-kiss and what a period and tampons were. Instead of dropping me off at the barn, my dad would reluctantly drop me off at my friend Lia's house after school to hang out. She had two older sisters who exposed us to Guns N' Roses and lingerie. They drank wine coolers and talked about sex, describing it as a boy doing push-ups over you. It sounded dumb.

I'd watch Lia's sisters sing along with their favorite songs blasting from the boom box, letting the beat vibrate through their bodies. They radiated power, energy, and a feistiness that felt risky and confident. It was like seeing wild horses in their element. We'd sit and watch them parade around in their bras and panties. For Halloween, one sister decided to be what she called "Underwear Man." She wore one pair of boy briefs as her underwear and another pair as a hat. She cut up an undershirt and wrote a "U" in sharpie on the back, then tied it around her neck as a cape. She wore a lacy black bra that held her large breasts high, and I couldn't help but stare at her.

As she was looking at herself in a full-length mirror, she caught my eye in the reflection. It startled me, her catching my glance, but even more startling was how breathtakingly attractive I found her. My gaze was interrupted when she called out to Lia, "Your friend is staring at me." I abruptly went to Lia's room and briefly wondered: *What was that all about?* Everyone found her mesmerizing. It wasn't weird that everyone included me, right?

The three sisters' lack of curfew and parental monitoring left us with a teen oasis. Their mom was often home watching TV downstairs in her pink robe. Her eyes were always damp. She would drink and smoke, and she'd randomly shout up to her daughters. She was barely present in her girls' lives or aware of what any of them might have needed. We'd avoid the living room she occupied and bring *Teen Vogue* magazines upstairs to the sisters' sanctuary, where we looked at fashion trends and completed the silly quizzes. It was a world of difference from my highly monitored life back home.

At this point, I had a sharp mouth and liked the way swear words came out sounding tough. I scared off some boys by demanding to see their bodies. I didn't really care much for physical interactions other than kissing and feeling around. I was figuring out my boundaries, practicing saying no, and being defiant and confident in my burgeoning womanhood. Which my parents—and particularly Ba—found alarming. Where had his innocent horse girl gone? I was wild and free; I was a force. Like Bart, I dared anyone to try to collect, contain, or hold me back.

Ma was deep in work mode. She was leading a team of a hundred software engineers with great success—people loved her leadership. Every now and then she'd re-enter a discussion about my curfew, which she always got wrong by an hour or two, forgetting what had been decided the year before. But Ba asked a lot of anxious questions and made up reasons why he couldn't give me a ride or wouldn't grant me permission to go out. He seemed terrified by my transition from Daddy's horse girl to this bold teenager—and convinced that somehow, I was doing this on purpose to hurt him. He was changing, mistrusting me, even trying to control me. In a way, Blackie's uncertain expression had been a forewarning. As if he somehow knew I would be stepping into an unsafe stall, a dangerous world, once I left the barn. As a young woman who looked different—*exotic*—a new kind of unshakeable target had been placed upon me.

Sally was the first horse I ever rode.

top Heading to a horse show in my barn-rat days.

bottom Every summer my days would begin and end in this hallway.

Competing in hunt seat equitation as a young tween.

5

ALL THE
HUNGRY
WOLVES

AFTER MY FIRST field hockey season wrapped up in late fall, I heard the local IHOP was hiring teenagers. For most of my childhood I had worked at the barn for free, so the thought of getting paid for labor was enticing. At the age of fourteen, I looked mature for my age. After my interview on a cold December afternoon, I was hired and given a uniform—a short, faded-blue dress with white ruffly sleeves and a sewn-on apron that made all the waitresses look like sexy handmaidens. I would work weekend and night shifts after school.

The older, popular girls I worked with wove in and out of my shifts. Some were nice and liked the attention we attracted. Some were mean and threatening. One particular girl wanted to beat me up because of her boyfriend's wandering eyes. Back at high school, she would walk the halls with her girl gang in search of me. When they located my classroom, she'd point at me with a determination and distaste that alarmed me. I had to choose my actions carefully once the bell rang and class was released. I needed to be calm, clear, and direct. No, I was not interested in her boyfriend. What football player? I didn't even know who he was. The fact that her boyfriend and his friends even noticed me seemed to fire up something inside her that I had to answer to.

Back at the restaurant, she ignored me as we focused on managing multiple tables for tips to supplement our low paychecks. Had we acted as a community, we would have had much more power and say over our working conditions, but we were divided—by station, by sections, by cliques, by popularity. Despite the dynamics at IHOP, I liked the challenge of remembering orders, anticipating requests, tallying up totals, and navigating multiple social interactions. Customers would come in with a blasé mood and my kind, engaging, even comedic approach often left them changed. My role as a server required a bit of performance. I approached each table with positivity and swiftness to keep at bay questions about my identity and where me and "my people" were from.

At the end of my shifts, I was tired and, again, smelled awful. To this day, I can still recall the smell of my little apron dress after a shift in the smoking section. Cigarettes, berry maple syrup, and burnt coffee are imprinted in my memory. Poor Ba. The winter nights he collected me from work, he'd plead with me not to take off my shoes in the car. "Ba, my feet are *so sore*! Please, can I just release the back of my heels?" I'd beg. My feet needed to be free. They had suffocated for hours in pantyhose and the stifling white sneakers we were required to wear. He'd roll down the driver-side window a tad to keep the chill out, hold his nose towards fresh air while slowly nodding, and brace himself. The stink was horrendous.

In some ways, IHOP was a show run by teenaged girls. Solo male customers eagerly sat in the smoking section at night to check us out. Once, a customer I served left a piece of paper with the room number at his hotel, which was close to the restaurant. He gave me an odd, hopeful look. I wasn't sure what to make of it.

I remember showing Ba the note when he picked me up. Ba went into a strange and quiet rage. It was the start of his panic about his daughter entering a world of men's desires, where he could not protect me yet still wanted to have control. I loved Ba and felt confused by his changing, reactive behavior. His supportive nature was being taken over by anxiety about no longer being able to control his teen daughter. My understanding of the concept of women needing protection, by men from men, began to unfold.

Around this time, I was scouted for a modeling opportunity, which required Ba and me to fly down to Atlanta, Georgia. It was exciting until I arrived at the convention. I felt concerned when I observed girls younger than me following around older men in charge, hoping to get noticed, to be chosen. It reminded me of that uncomfortable part of being in the show ring—of having to perform and look the part, to sell your talent to make yourself seem worthy, selectable. It's not what I wanted. I decided to leave the scouting event early and Ba was proud of me. So, we left. It was probably a scam anyway.

DURING MY high school years, different groups of friends wove in and out of my life. I gravitated towards befriending boys, but then if they developed feelings and I didn't reciprocate, the friendship would end. It was confusing and hurtful. I wanted to experience a level playing field with my peers, not reside in uncertainty over what was real friendship. It seemed that people always had an underlying motive, and once it showed itself, I either became a scapegoat or lost a friend. When I had a crush on someone, I wanted to be in charge of my sexuality and desire. When I felt desire, it was electric. Yet when I was desired, I felt exposed and uncomfortable. I couldn't trust the person's intentions and I felt overwhelmed by how the media and society overly sexualized women and girls. The message we received as girls was that men were in charge and what they wanted mattered. Men were like hungry wolves eyeing you, waiting for an opportunity when you were separated from your herd. I longed for a girl gang. I felt like I had to appear tough. It seemed that as a woman, safety was never a guarantee—you had to protect yourself from men.

Gram, who was held back in so many ways by men in her life, had been groomed to serve—much like I was at IHOP. One weekend while she was over, she handed me a vintage booklet after I'd returned from the brunch shift. The title was written in a poppy, angled font: *Pies Men Like*.

I laughed. "Gram, this is hilarious! Wow, what a relic."

She frowned and pursed her lips. That wasn't the reaction she expected. "I think this is important for you to know, that your place... is in... the kitchen."

I was exasperated. She was serious. This wasn't a joke.

"Gram, my place is not in the kitchen! It's out in the world. I'm going to go to college and get an education, get a career, and experience life. Live boldly."

Her expression transitioned. A painful memory seemed to hover over her concerned expression, the one I remembered from the tickling sessions of my childhood. She asked me, as if someone else was talking for her: "Why would you want to go to college?"

I looked at her and felt empathy soothe my initial defensiveness. I understood—the concept of a woman going to college was both intriguing and daunting to her. An unknown. And making pies, which the pamphlet offered recipes for, is what she knew and what she could offer me. I gave her a hug.

"Gram," I responded in a gentle voice, "that's what we do now, it's our time."

She looked up at me, as if to nod. I could feel the slice of otherness that we shared, however different the flavor and mix might be. I thought of all the hungry wolves that take, take, take. And how much they'd taken from her. It served as a warning to me to stand my ground. I hoped that in my embrace, away from the world of men and the pies they liked, away from harm and cruelty, she'd feel safe, seen, and free.

Just then I heard rumbling coming from outside: a thunderstorm brewed in the distance. It was foreboding, as if to warn that the moment of feeling safe, seen, and free would be fleeting—not just for Gram, but for me, too.

I hoped that in my embrace, away from the cruel world of men and the pies they liked, Gram would feel safe, seen, and free.

IN THE SPRING of my freshman year, I acquired an older boyfriend, with his own car. And it seemed to really catapult my parents, especially my dad, into a frenzy. As a teenager, I dug my heels in and revolted against their attempts to hold me back. Ba had begun asking a lot of questions about my knowledge of boys and even sex, which felt inappropriate and confusing, and I caught him covertly listening to my conversations on the landline. He overreacted a lot and even cried when my headstrong nature wore him down.

Ba didn't seek out therapy or a coach, but he did seek support from the church's male groups. I knew these men were bad news. Half of them were porn obsessed. They were the wolves in sheep's clothing the pastor talked about most Sundays. Even my little brother's ten-year-old friends were asking if he had ever seen me naked. Everyone who feared Lucifer was sitting right next to him; to a young person, that was clear as day. I was exoticized, especially as a teenager, by men in the congregation who would then use me as a scapegoat. In their minds, perhaps it was the way I dressed that caused this unwanted desire. But they had no business looking at me in the way they did or treating me like I was the problem. I strongly disagreed with the messages we were taught in church.

Whether or not it was the fault of his failed church group, Ba was angry at me for growing up. For changing. For wanting to direct my own power and sexuality. In this heartbreaking way, I had to realize that Ba wasn't separate from the world of men. He was a part of it and knew it so well he was now engulfed in its darkness. His beautiful daughter, the catalyst of so much desire, had to be contained, maybe even destroyed.

In the throes of his obsession, Ba followed me and my boyfriend to his parents' empty house one night that same summer. I had said we were going out to a diner, but on the way there my boyfriend suggested we go hang out at his house. There was no threat in his suggestion, and I agreed. It was thrilling! And it was a chance to connect away from overt adult supervision. As if my boyfriend sensed that we might be followed, he parked on the back street behind his parents' house.

Soon after we arrived, sure enough, a car pulled up the driveway. The headlights beamed up and over the windows of the upstairs room we were in. My boyfriend turned off the lamp and we just sat on the floor, scared. The car door opened and closed. We heard someone take a few steps, followed by a fist banging on the front door. I startled when I heard my dad's voice, shouting my name in a way that did not sound like him. It was as if Ba had become the lead character in *The Shining*. It terrified us into silence, and we sat frozen. He moved what sounded like a heavy flowerpot to the edge of the garage and then there was a series of scratching noises getting louder and louder. A moment later, there he was, glaring at us through the open window, his head framed by the opaque curtains flowing in the blue moonlight.

"Go downstairs, right now," he demanded, as he turned to go down and meet us at the front door.

What was initially shock and disbelief transformed into anger, shooting through my veins. *Did Dad just climb up the wall and crawl across the roof to the window?* I had *had* it. I ran downstairs, opened the front door, and lifted my finger at him.

"Don't you hurt him," I commanded.

I turned around and bolted through the back door. I wanted to run so far away from this oppressive power that I had to fight, confront, and protect myself from. I ran until I crossed a short bridge and was out of breath. It was a warm night, and I was wearing shorts and a tank top. I heard a car turn on and drive slowly past me. In the front seats, two older men turned to stare at me. I suddenly felt exposed, alone in the night, pursued by men in cars scanning the streets. They kept driving past me but by the next block they had started to turn around.

My instinct was to hide. I felt unsafe, like they were coming for me. My heart was beating through my throat, concealing a scream. I considered my options, determined to get out of harm's way. There was a fire station across the street with a circle of thick bushes in front of it. I sprinted to the bushes and hid, just in time to watch the headlights of the car scan the area. They circled slowly, as if hunting prey. In that moment, I realized that running away wouldn't be the path to my liberation, especially not as a teen girl. Men dominated the outside world; they made it dangerous.

After what felt like an eternity, the two men in the car gave up looking for me. When they left, I darted out of the bushes, running back the way I came, over the bridge, my heart leaping out of my chest. I wished I was riding Blackie so that I could get away from this place. On the other side of the bridge was a closed gas station with a pay phone on the side of the garage. I gripped the phone and used a collect call to ring my boyfriend's landline. He picked up. I explained where I was, that I was being followed, and told him to get there as fast as possible. It was the longest few minutes I ever waited. His car skidded into the station, and I jumped in, shaking. He drove me back to his parents' home, where Ba was waiting for me.

The next thing I knew, I was riding in the backseat of Ba's Volvo. Through the rearview mirror, I watched him looking at the road. So much had changed between us. Our trust was broken. I yearned for him to be open with me, to be vulnerable, to be curious about learning who I was becoming. I wanted him to ask me what I needed. This kind of discipline only had one outcome: disconnection. We remained silent for the entire drive home, until suddenly, unprompted, he stated: "I won't tell your mother about this." At the time, I wished he would. She was perhaps the only person who could see through the sexist, predatory maze I was engulfed in.

WHEN THAT SUMMER ENDED, my parents announced that I wouldn't be returning to my high school that fall. I had been enrolled in an all-girls private school in Princeton, New Jersey. My dad had paid a lot of money to keep me away from boys and men—particularly my boyfriend. Having no say in the matter, I was angry and upset. Once it settled in that I had no choice, I was depressed. Every day, Ba drove me to my new school. I tried out for field hockey and only made junior varsity. The girlfriends I had back at public school were starting rumors about me, frustrated about my departure. The new girlfriends I made were all quite wealthy and had their own coping mechanisms to deal with their parents and society: drugs and raves.

Looking back, I enjoyed the all-girls school. I just couldn't stand being excluded from the decision-making process. And I recoiled from the school's religious component. It was Catholic and nuns walked around with a ruler, measuring the height of our skirts. Mine, from Contempo Casuals, were always too short. But the quality of the education was amazing. This school was where I was first introduced to photography. I fought hard with my parents to return to public school and won, unfortunately. By the time I returned, for the winter term of my sophomore year, I was so ahead in all subjects that I was put in advanced placement courses. I had teachers at the Catholic school who saw my depression and encouraged me to immerse myself in science, math, literature, and art. I had never read so many books in one term. My photography teacher showed me the work of Barbara Kruger and other feminist artists, which was key to who I'd become in the future.

Walking back through the bleak halls of my public high school felt different. It was clear to me that my former friends weren't my friends any longer. Whatever rumors they had started, they couldn't stop or fix, even though they wanted to. I was tired of girls who chose boys over our friendship. I was tired of the popularity game, the mean-girl culture, and the unrelenting power of gossip. The field hockey team was no longer my team, given I had spent the fall on an entirely different private-school track. I snowboarded with a small group of guys throughout the winter and by the spring, I broke up with my boyfriend and began skateboarding after school. I was lonely.

I found solace in fashion, secondhand shopping, self-expression, music, and art. I was drawn to the art wing of school and to science and math classes—amazed at how physics and spatial thinking were so visual. Ma was selected to attend a summer program for executive women at Smith College, and, thanks to her encouragement, I joined a program in science for teenage girls that would overlap with her program. Being in northwestern Massachusetts that summer was beautiful. I met androgynous girls and boys whom I was drawn to. I even got my belly button pierced and snuck out of my dorm room with my dormmates to make out with pretty boys while listening to the band Mazzy Star. I walked by my resident assistant's room and saw another college-aged girl lying on top of her, and they were kissing. For a moment I thought about how amazing that must feel, how comfortable I was with that scene, and then filed it away. I was about to meet up with my girl gang, most of whom attended the arts program while I was making instruments and learning about lasers and human psychology. Even though Ma and I didn't meet up much that summer, it felt good to know she had her own girl gang of executives on campus whom she was bonding with.

BACK FROM our respective programs, I spent the rest of the summer before junior year eager to get my license to gain more independence, while Ma doubled down on her commitment to church. She would pretend like we had a choice whether to go to church, as she wanted us to *want* to go. But when we resisted, she would use guilt trips and disappointment to manipulate us into accompanying her.

One Sunday morning, my driver's license finally in hand, I put up a fight about not going to church. I'd much rather go on a joy ride! Jon was with me. But Ma shot me an intense, even frantic look. She gripped my arm and dug her nails into my skin, demanding, "Why can't you be an obedient daughter?" It shook me, I could feel so much of her anger, her energy, blow into me as if I were a thin reed in the wind. Giving up having a choice meant giving her what she wanted. And so, I gave that to her.

When we arrived, I couldn't sit still in the pew. I couldn't sing the harmonies in the morning songs. I needed space, needed to give myself what I needed, not just be expected to give it away to my parents. I looked at Ma, catching her attention. I asked to borrow her car, that I'd forgotten something, and I'd pick her and the family up after. She frowned. I persisted and she reluctantly handed me the keys to her Subaru. The impact of her disappointed expression was short lived. Leaving the church was as exhilarating as that long trail ride back to our old housing development. Oh, what joy it was to leave!

The sun was shining. It was a hot summer day. I was giddy skipping, then running to the car. I had it all to myself! I turned the ignition, blasted the air conditioner, and turned on the radio to find a song that matched my energy. I spun out of the church parking lot like a bat out of hell. I was free.

But on the way home, a spider that had made its way into the car caught the air conditioning stream and blew right into my face. It immediately brought me back to Gram and spider crickets! I frantically wiped my face to get it off, and by the time I looked up again, the road had curved but the car hadn't. Like Bart at that final jump, I had missed the signal. I swerved quickly and the car spun out of control, colliding with a massive tree at the edge of a river. I came to, this time my vision focusing on white dust particles around me. The airbag had activated, thankfully. And right in front of the deflated air bag was a tree. I realized then that if it weren't for that airbag, I would have flown through the windshield and into the tree. My seat belt was slightly off my shoulder; I could have died.

A nonverbal policeman treated me like a stupid teenaged girl and drove me home. I quickly called the church to inform my parents that I had been in a car accident and was now home. It felt like forever, but when they finally arrived, Ma didn't rush to see if I was okay. I *appeared* fine and so instead, as punishment for smashing her car, she didn't talk to me for two weeks. In fact, she never talked to me about that day or the accident.

Ba checked in on me, but by then I was uncomfortable around him. His anger, that I had grown up and was no longer his little girl, turned to harming me for the pain and betrayal I had caused him. He even used helping my mother as a form of manipulation, which generated deep scars for me as a teen, and, as an added effect, widened the distance between me and Ma. I felt I had to shield her from these experiences. I couldn't trust nor guarantee that if exposed, she'd choose to protect and comfort me over my father.

The fall entering my junior year I felt lonely and depressed. But, to my relief, when a new skater girl transferred to my high school spring of my junior year, and we immediately became best frirends, that loneliness was replaced with joy and connection. KC was fun, confident, and kind. After quitting my job at IHOP—I couldn't take the maple syrup, male clientele, and those stinky shoes any longer—I got an after-school job as a stylist at Contempo Casuals in the local mall. KC and I would always meet up afterwards to skate in the parking garage.

One day after classes wrapped and our afternoon was free, we sat on the bumper of my uncle's hand-me-down, beat-up Honda Civic, and she shared something that took me by surprise.

"What's up?" I asked.

"I have to... tell you something."

She fidgeted a bit, adjusting her posture, and gazed out somewhere beyond the high school parking lot. Her attention shifted to her shoes and the asphalt beneath their soles. Her eyes hovered over to my shoes and then slowly floated up towards my face.

"I, I haven't always dated boys," she said nervously, immediately averting her eyes.

I waited for her to continue.

"I had a girlfriend," she explained. She looked at me with anticipation.

I could see she was hoping I wouldn't be weirded out. Yes, it caught me by surprise. I had never considered the possibility of dating girls. I thought about the one goth couple in school, two girls who leaned up against their lockers, kissing one another while the taller one wrapped her arms around the other girl's neck. I reflected on that dorm-room scene, one girl lying on top of another. I thought it was beautiful and brave, but I never extended that possibility to myself nor to my friends.

Looking at KC and her vulnerability through her anxious eyes, I told her that being bisexual didn't bother me, not in the slightest. I was curious about her experience, but I kept that to myself, somewhere deep and difficult to find. She took a breath, looked down again and back out beyond the parking lot, then at me. She smiled out of the corner of her mouth.

"I'm so glad you're not weirded out." She exhaled and rubbed her hands together to shake off the perspiration that had gathered.

That night after skateboarding and joy riding, she asked if she could sleep over. This was new, but okay, why not? We went back to my house. My parents were in one of their overly dramatic moods and, with little explanation, steadfast against the idea of a sleepover. My parents and I constantly battled over our kaleidoscope of needs, none of which were met. It was a disheartening and crushing time.

In this instance with KC, I pushed back and questioned their reasons. *Why can't she sleep over?* KC was standing in the entranceway. Out of exhaustion from the bickering, perhaps out of embarrassment, they changed their minds and agreed that she could stay over. I didn't understand what they were so up in arms about. But maybe they sensed that this friend could be *more* than a friend. That night we shared my little twin bed. It was exciting to have her there—comforting, even protective. I thought about the girl skater gang from a neighboring school that she had recently introduced me to. How they held such collective confidence and a camaraderie I yearned for. It was as if every smack of their boards and whiz of wheels on asphalt drummed up the sound of teenage rebellion. They were making a space momentarily free from social, familial, and gendered expectations and limitations. Girls are powerful.

As I drifted in my own thoughts, KC rolled over in her sleep and spooned me, cuddling and holding me close. It caught me a bit off guard, it was so foreign. Her arms felt strong, yet soft. I felt strands of her hair meshing with mine along my neck. She exhaled lightly as if she, too, felt incredibly safe. I wondered when, if ever, I would feel this again.

Nothing ever happened between us beyond friendship. Yet even that phased out. It was a common pattern. I was sensitive, and I had one too many experiences where eventually a friend would—as Ma would say—let me down. I easily felt misunderstood, rejected, betrayed. Meanwhile, I could imagine my friends' point of view: I was desired and popular. What could I feel unhappy about? I hadn't met another mixed-race woman, and I wanted to. I was so grateful I had my little brother to connect with, but he was quite young. I didn't know how to ask him whether he was experiencing similar things. Was he being exoticized? Was he feeling seen? Did he feel like he belonged? And if so, where and with whom? Throughout my remaining teen years, I sought a ballast to keep me afloat. I found it in music, in women's movements, and in moments of curiosity and connection with strangers.

THE SUMMER BEFORE my senior year, Jon—who was eleven—and I joined our parents for another family visit in Taipei. As usual, stepping out from Nai Nai's apartment into the city streets felt like an adventure and a throwback to my childhood. Except that now, anytime Jon and I went to pay for something, someone would make a comment about our appearance during the exchange. I noticed that in public, we were looked at, stared at, even. It was as if my brother and I were celebrities, but why, we weren't sure.

I no longer felt the freedom of going unseen and just being at my home away from home. I felt off kilter, like a stranger, like I had been granted a superiority I did not ask for or earn. People would say, "So beautiful, so Western-looking," and I humbly thanked them for the compliment. "Xie xie, bu hao yi si." Thank you, you shouldn't have.

I worried that my Western features only served to reinforce the trend of double-eyelid surgeries and bleaching products marketed to Asian women who wanted to look more Caucasian. All around me I saw the influence of westernization creep into my culture, and I wanted to protect it. Yet I knew that how I *appeared* might as well be a walking advertisement, no matter what I tried to do to thwart it.

Given all the attention I was getting, Ma asked my aunt if she could arrange an interview for me with one of the modeling agencies in Taipei. The irony was that I was the second-shortest woman in my Asian family at five feet six. Ma was the shortest at five feet five. All our female relatives stood between five feet, seven inches, and five feet, nine inches tall. Despite my height limitations, my aunt made the call and an appointment was set.

I sought a ballast to keep me afloat. I found it in music, in women's movements, and in moments of curiosity and connection.

Ma came with me given that my Mandarin was now quite limited; as a young adult, I knew only as much as I'd learned as a five-year-old. I felt dependent on her and uneasy. Mid-shoot, the photographer said I had mature eyes and a strong spirit. Whether that was a direct translation, or what Ma wanted him to say, I wasn't surprised by that observation. I had been through a lot already in my short, young life.

As the meeting wrapped, the agent offered me a one-year contract with the caveat that I would have to move to Taipei. That possibility sunk in. If I accepted the offer, I'd be alone. Having my family with me was reassuring and an important part of my time spent in the country. And I relied on Ma. Without her, I might feel lost. I imagined days of boredom, moments of confusion, and performing based on my looks. The memory of equestrian training crept into my mind—I saw myself falling off Bart, I recalled how my trainer didn't ask if I was okay, and I remembered the expectation to perform. This felt like another role I'd have to play.

I thought about my value being intrinsically tied to that role. I thought about seeing myself on a billboard in the future, my face associated with a particular product being advertised. I thought about how I wanted to make an impact on the world, on society, for other young people and girls like me. I wanted to lead a purpose-driven life and the idea of being on my own at a young age didn't sit right with me. I let Ma know how I felt, and she was supportive. I wanted a different kind of attention, even if there was glamour and allure in modeling. I wanted to figure out who I was and who I was becoming. There was still so much to untangle, to learn and understand.

As we rode in a taxi back to my grandmother's apartment, I looked over at Ma and then out at the active city. I looked beyond the high-rises at the mountains in the distance. I thought about how Ma was the only person in my Asian family who understood my bicultural experience. I thought about how she so effectively translated for me, and how she relied on me to speak "good English" back at home. How she always wanted me to read passages out loud from the Bible to her and remarked how well I spoke. Yet in comparison, she had mastered two languages, which she was both fluent and literate in. My mother, who remarked that I was "more beautiful than Mommy," believed my command of English and my Caucasian features were valuable currency, regardless of my language barriers and limitations in her own home country.

I looked at her remarkable face and thought about how much I valued and loved her. In that moment, I wondered why I had never told her about that night I ran away, after Ba confronted me at that boy's house and the car of men followed me. If I brought it up, would she blame me for it? Would she have helped Ba realize me growing up wasn't a betrayal and untwist his twisted sense of possession over me? I couldn't risk the possibility of her rejection, of feeling unworthy, misunderstood, and abandoned. So I said nothing.

My brother and I in 1994.

The pamphlet Gram gave me about pies men like.

五
TWISTED IN DESIRE

Ma wasn't thrilled when I chose UMass Amherst as the college I would attend for my freshman year. For one, it was out-of-state tuition; and second, she felt it was much too far for me to live away from home. However, it had an equine science veterinary program that I found appealing and, come August, I found myself saying my goodbyes to my family in my dorm room—a cinder block–walled, tiny room with two twin bunk beds. As my family left, Ma instructed me to drive home most weekends. But I felt a new sense of freedom as they departed. I was no longer under the rule and thumb of my strict parents.

My first semester was filled with completing coursework and meeting new friends, having crushes, and even getting a bad case of food poisoning. I visited my family often—the long four-to-five-hour drives from campus to central New Jersey were tiring. Like I had during my teen experience at Smith College, I began gravitating towards the visual arts and away from the sciences.

I skated to classes and confidently argued with my professors about animal ethics after observing practices I didn't agree with. I realized that perhaps being a vet wasn't for me. And so, for my second term, I selected courses in arts and humanities. I let my advanced courses in chemistry and mathematics take a back seat, feeling that my choices were getting me closer to identifying what I wanted to learn, where I wanted to grow as a young woman.

You can imagine, then, my shock when I turned up to the registrar's office to select fall courses for my sophomore year and the attendant announced, "You're no longer a student at the university." I stood there confused, not able to speak. "You are marked as withdrawn. Unenrolled," they explained. I thought of all the reasons why I might be unenrolled. Clearly, there had to be some mistake. As they waited for my response, they returned to their computer screen, clacking at the keyboard.

"Appears that you were unenrolled as of last week, by... your guardian."

I was stunned. Humiliated. Completely disempowered. At that moment, I knew which guardian it was: Ma. She had made this decision and never bothered to tell me. We were back here again: Forcing me to go to church on Sundays. Pulling me out of public high school. A pattern that said my parents were in charge and consulting me was unnecessary. I wished that one of my parents would simply ask me what my needs were and be honest, tell me about what was on their mind, what was at the center of the issue.

Despite the many opportunities Ma had on the weekends I drove down to spend time with family, there had been no discussion or open conversation. Unenrolling me from the school I had chosen for myself took the wind right out of my newfound sails. I confronted Ma. She admitted, without any sign of regret or apology, that she had forged my signature and enrolled me at Douglass College, an all-female public school at Rutgers University, where I was to attend in the fall. I tried explaining to her how I had made friends at school and was looking forward to going back. She informed me that her investment in an out-of-state school was solely tied to my interest in equine science. I had decided not to become a veterinarian, and so, to Ma, that meant I would no longer attend UMass. Douglass was closer and would save money since she and Ba could pay in-state tuition. I was deeply appreciative of their investment in my education. However, not being able to find my own way into courses that interested me so that I could explore my future direction in life was debilitating. Why go to college if your parents are going to dictate the experience for you, based on what they choose, expect, or want?

Reluctantly, I packed up my dorm-room belongings and said goodbye to friends and a relatively new relationship. Looking back through the rearview mirror at the beautiful landscape of Western Massachusetts, I felt like I was driving away from the future and back into the past. Everyone else was moving forward, as I returned home, falling backwards.

THAT SUMMER at home, I was depressed. Ma assumed that, with the proximity of Douglass College, I'd just keep living at my parents' house when classes started in the fall. I felt trapped by the idea. At home, Ba was still missing his little girl, a version of me I had abruptly abandoned. Ma was a bit unhinged and expressed her disapproval in how we, her kids, were turning out. She'd cry to my brother and me that our foul language and joking manner reminded her that we'd never make it into the kingdom of God and be with her in the afterlife. My brother was now a thirteen-year-old who embraced punk rock. He looked like Sid Vicious, smoked and drank, and had a never-ending crew of groupies awaiting any signs of interest from him. I could see my brother rebelling. Every eight-inch spike of his hair was a protective boundary from the expectations that bombarded him. I totally got it. Ma could cut us both down with the disappointment of her unfilled expectations. To her, everything we did impacted how she was perceived, which had become very important to her.

There was no sanctuary for us, set up to gather ourselves in. At our home, boundaries were meant to be broken.

As much as I wanted to spend time with my brother, I was desperate to get out of the house. It had become a space of extreme discomfort, of suffocation. I craved a bigger pasture where I could reconnect with my essence, which was what it seemed like everyone else in my age group was able to do. In my home environment, it was like I was bound, held from growing up and becoming myself. It was as if my parents were terrified of the power that my full self might yield and that I needed to be protected from. They never explained it in this way. It was a cryptic, underlying message I absorbed when I found their reactions too dumbfounding to follow.

Thankfully, near the end of that restless, tumultuous summer, my parents agreed to let me rent a room off campus in New Brunswick. I was relieved. I researched and found a few promising room rental listings on a new platform called Craigslist. Ba and Jon took me to check them out. Ba could tell I was miserable at home. My presence wasn't contributing to the kind of happy nuclear family he and Ma craved, and perhaps, needed. Their desire to have this picture-perfect family seemed connected to justifying all their hardships and difficulties—proving their choices had been worth it. I needed a moment's peace from the intersecting cultural collisions and identity crisis that had us mixed-race kids breathing the fumes of our parents' angst and disappointment.

THAT FIRST TERM at Douglass, I slowly began making a few friends. My housemates were a funny bunch. One of them, Loren, was a tall blonde with big breasts who was studying photography and architecture. I loved how she was both awkward and beautiful. She seemed like she didn't quite fit the body she was born into. She was nerdy and if you got her to laugh, she'd crescendo into a colossal expression of joy. She and I got along and cooked together a lot. She could handle spicy food, unlike our other housemates, and she didn't hold back on getting second helpings at dinner, which was usually followed by our favorite dessert: store-bought angel food cake, strawberries, and whipped cream. I liked our dinner rituals, just the two of us. We talked about our classes, growing up feeling different, and navigating stereotypes. We enjoyed each other's company.

Xenophobia was not my crux to bear alone. It was shared by many. We had a history of challenging oppression, working towards liberation, and creating culture, bit by bit.

Loren lived on the second floor of the house and shared a bathroom with another blonde who was allergic to washing dishes. I rented a private room in the attic with a small bathroom. It was my refuge, just what the doctor would have ordered if I'd been in therapy. I had a campus meal plan, and I explored the various campus mess halls and café options. On Thursdays, I discovered a secret deal where, for five dollars, students with meal cards could enjoy a full dinner at the Rutgers Club. I let a few friends in on the secret and we'd gather to have a nice meal with soup, salad, a main course, dessert, and coffee. We felt smart and grown-up.

Much like Ma when she traveled to other countries, I explored the campus using the public transportation system. I'd walk to the train station that connected students and professors alike to New York City and Princeton. I registered for a Chinese calligraphy class and a painting course I was intrigued by that brought me to the Mason Gross School of the Arts. The more exploring I could do and the more choices I could make for myself, the better.

My women's and gender studies course was mandatory, though I couldn't have chosen better. It was in a typical classroom with chairs connected to desks, all facing the front chalkboard, with a small TV stand and VCR player in the corner. The walls were a light green palette, and the frosted windows at the back of the room cast a glow onto the eyeglasses of my young female professor's face. The readings were rigorous and contained a flood of information that was new to me. Every source gave language and meaning to the pain and suffering I had experienced—racialized sexism, exoticization, and othering. I read about the social history of women, the fight for women's rights, and the inequity we all face as people of color—beacons of truth so bright I could barely read the words radiating off the page. This knowledge was something I had yearned for, needed, and wanted. And yet, my initial reaction was shock. I felt flustered.

Why had this information been so inaccessible in my life up until now? So hidden from my reach, and yet so accessible and present in this classroom setting? I read stories spanning decades of action, public art, political impact, and theoretical discourse on the systems of oppression I had navigated. Nineteen years earlier on the same campus, my parents met and fell in love. They boldly lived in choice—choosing one another, placing aside the otherness and spotlight their interracial relationship drew upon them. Given the close physical proximity that connected my world now with my parents' world then, I was astounded by my lack of exposure to this rich history of resistance. As I walked out that classroom, near the hospital where I was born, I felt like roaring. I demanded to see the manager.

My teacher—a kind, young, and hip feminist—recognized my turmoil and tended to my new awakenings. Her eyes were wise and exuded warmth and understanding. She responded to my papers and met me where I was without judgement, with the patience of a wise elder. She gave me out-of-the-box assignments so I could explore and surf the wave of every feminist movement I had hungrily read about and felt connected to.

What soon replaced my initial anger was passion. Another shift was happening inside me. An embrace. Gratitude.

Even a promise. This was the clarity I needed around the dynamics I was seeing, experiencing, and facing as a young person growing up. Xenophobia was not my crux to bear alone. It was one shared by many, and we had a history of challenging oppression, working towards liberation, and creating culture, bit by bit. My lens was expanding. I was connecting the dots of who I was in the context of race, gender, and identity. And I was beginning to see how my positionality was a gift I could use in transformative ways.

Gram's pie pamphlet, as thin as it was, had a force to it. I had felt its weight, which Gram and her generation had little choice but to succumb to. It was like the dark matter surrounding, connecting, and separating us across a matrix of power, otherness, and social norms. I sensed the fray of this dynamic across my fraught and fractured relationships with other women my age. I wanted to alleviate the gravitational pull of this dynamic we existed in, where boys and men were at the center.

While I was learning and connecting all of this, I was given a class assignment on gender representation. I spent the day dressed up in a suit and tie and observed the different, new attention I received—the curious looks, the stares. I examined how I felt being seen in this new way, which wasn't due primarily to my mixed-race otherness but to the remix of my gender presentation. I felt an undercurrent of danger tugging me in one direction, while the force of convention pulled in the other, urging me to quickly change back to the safer outfit, a more femininized option. I lingered, observed, questioned this intersectional dimension. Women who present more masculine are incredibly bold, and sexy. I chuckled to myself. I wonder what kind of pie *she* likes.

I started to see that so much of how we present ourselves in society is, in fact, a performance. I learned from John Berger's *Ways of Seeing* about the impact of being seen versus being heard. Men, without question, were the subject and women, by default, were the object being observed and acted upon. I loved reading work by powerful women of color and trans and queer scholars of this time. In *Ain't I a Woman*, bell hooks wrote, "To me feminism is not simply a struggle to end male chauvinism or a movement to ensure that women will have equal rights with men; it is a commitment to eradicating the ideology of domination that permeates Western culture on various levels—sex, race, and class." *Yes, yes, yes a thousand times yes.* She wrote that when I was one year old. She, like all the scholars, theorists, artists, activists, and women of color in union across racial and gendered lines, of the past and present, was part of the community to which I *finally* belonged.

I am a *feminist*. Thanks, Ma, for forging my signature. You were right, after all.

IN THE SPRING TERM of my sophomore year, I took an intro to art history course. As I made my way through the history books written predominantly by men, I connected the dots of female artists in Asia, Europe, the Americas, Mexico, and beyond. I was drawn to Artemisia Gentileschi, Rosa Bonheur, Camille Claudel, Frida Kahlo, and then, the period that became my favorite: the 1960s-to-1980s feminist art history era. I loved this era, where women came together in community, using art to expand perspectives and shift what bell hooks would call the white-supremacist capitalist patriarchy's status quo. I remembered as a teen girl that photography teacher introducing me to the work of Barbara Kruger. Her piece *Untitled (Your Body Is a Battleground)* spoke volumes.

I soon made the decision to pursue a double major in art history and women's and gender studies. In my research, I was enamored with the mixed-race artist Adrian Piper. She played with her identity by performing in public to generate discomfort in the viewer. In one of her public works series called *Catalysis*, named after her ability to catalyze audiences, she traveled in the subway with a cloth in her mouth that she had soaked in cod oil. I wondered if this was her response to the confrontational questions of "What are you?" and "Where are your people from?"

She designed installations, such as *Cornered* in 1988, to confront xenophobia and address the onlooker directly about the history of miscegenation in America as an example of cultural bias and the impact it has on an individual. This piece spoke to me about the ways we can engage in shifting mindsets and connecting across difference. It also reminded me that, having felt trapped like an exotic animal in a patriarchal zoo, I had the power to step out, to inform, to get my power back in spades.

I continued taking painting classes at Mason Gross. I could feel the paint, connect with my emotions, and experiment with the message I wanted to convey. I coordinated an art show of my work at the women's and gender studies department. Several students and professors commented on my work and a few even purchased pieces. Being among fellow creative types, including many who had experienced feeling like an outsider, was comforting.

It made sense that from art, music would follow. With my power returning, I was getting my voice back, too. The Christmas of my sophomore year, my parents gifted me what has become one of my favorite presents: a vintage PA sound system, mic stand, and microphone. I already played the piano, and I started learning guitar and writing lyrics and melody. I thought about Björk and The Cranberries—how much I admired these musicians, belting out their stories in ways that helped me sort out my feelings, soaring alongside their harmonies. I found out about the Riot Grrrl movement in the 1990s—the decade I entered as a ten-year-old and exited in my twenties—when feminist musicians formed iconic bands like Bikini Kill and Le Tigre in the Pacific Northwest and addressed sexism as a girl riot, giving girls their power back.

In my art class, I made friends with a goofy, shy illustrator named Brad who looked like George from the Beatles. He was a guitar player. As we painted in the studio, I told him, "I play keys, and I sing. I have a sound system and a mic. Want to jam sometime?" We started writing songs together.

It didn't take very long to start a band, and two additional friends joined on bass and drums. That summer we created the indie rock band World Without Maps. We were a group of creatives committed to writing and practicing songs together. We rehearsed in my apartment's living room until we got too loud. Surprisingly, my parents

I am a feminist.
Thanks, Ma,
for forging my
signature. You were
right, after all.

suggested we practice in their basement, to bring their daughter back home. It must have been hard for my parents to think or engage in conversation as the music shook beneath them. Yet they never complained and always welcomed us back. They listened as we belted out lyrics on our microphones over the competing sound of the drumkit and amps.

The bass player and I would get into charged academic arguments on a weekly basis. I often found that he—maybe subconsciously—ganged up on me with the other boys by his side. I was tired of feeling like our conversations were a competition to see who was smarter. He, the Philosopher and Linguist, versus me, the Feminist and Art Historian. That feeling continued onstage, where we'd eventually perform for a live audience.

I wondered: *Am I the token woman in the band?* I wasn't entirely comfortable being onstage. I felt stared at, analyzed. My male bandmates all seemed so confident. They were comfortable in this space they had the privilege of occupying, where perhaps they felt they belonged. My relationship with the stage would need nurturing. To get up onstage and be seen, to be the subject, was an act of bravery. I couldn't step fully into that space that my little kid self had once occupied so freely. The stage was not yet a place where I felt like I belonged.

Our indie rock band got billed at local shows and on the college radio station. We even got a free studio recording session at Princeton University that produced a cassette tape of our songs. World Without Maps was an opportunity for me to take up space in a male-dominated arena.

Although our music was rough and often sounded like two competing singers at odds with one another, most of the time we had a blast. As bandmates, we were all in.

Brad and I started dating. For a time, it was a beautiful partnership. We were best friends, bandmates, creatives, and lovers. We made art, sang, explored New York City's art museums and galleries, and enjoyed one another's company. We had silly names for one another, enjoyed afternoon breaks, worked on papers side by side, and had dinner with each other's families. Of course, Ma didn't really think he was up to snuff, but that was no different from her opinion of any other boyfriend I'd had, so on it went. Until it didn't.

The first signal of something shifting was at a house party. Our band had just played, and the bassist's crush was there, Siouxsie. I had never noticed how big her brown eyes were, and we kept catching one another's glances. She had a beautiful figure. Her short black hair looked as though she had just stepped out of a Vidal Sassoon workshop. She was striking and mysterious. I looked over at her as the floorboards creaked from people dancing to the music. Caught up in the moment, I walked over, gently collected her hand in mine, and guided her to the makeshift dance floor. She smiled at me as we slow danced, our bodies pressed together, ignoring the stares and whispers. My bandmates were seated just past us, mouths agape, but I could see only the shine of her lip gloss.

I leaned in and welcomed what became my first-ever girl kiss. Her mouth was soft, her lips full, pressing and widening onto mine. I felt connected and alive. I wrapped my arm around her waist and kept kissing her, as if this was the first time I had ever kissed anyone before. She was confident and sensual and leaned in to me. I was surprised to feel a hunger inside me, a rapture for more. I imagined the whole room empty and me and Siouxsie making our way to my bedroom. And then, it was over.

She gently detached herself and walked back to the bass player to pick up their earlier conversation. Brad, my best friend and lover, joined me on the dance floor, but things had changed for me. What just happened? Where did that moment go? It was as if everyone moved on, leaving me spellbound on the dance floor. Before the party ended, I caught up with Siouxsie as she was leaving and said, "Hey, we should hang out." She looked at me, smiled, and gave me her number.

A few weeks later, Brad and I broke up. He had found his way into the arms of another crush he had, and somehow, I felt used. As if through me, he had gained the confidence and mojo to date other women. I was heartbroken and felt washed up, tossed aside. The band suffered through our breakup, which marked the beginning of the end for World Without Maps.

Eventually, I called Siouxsie and she ended up in my bedroom. I was excited, surprised, and uncertain about how this would play out. We had hung out late and she suggested sleeping over. A blue hue of light cascaded across her face through my window. My bed was simply a mattress on the floor, which grounded us in this intimate scene. But, out of nowhere, once we laid down she silently turned around. I looked at the back of her head, now facing me. I caught a scent of her pheromones, which was riveting. I was the big spoon waiting for her to turn over and make out, leading us to touch, feel, and explore our bodies. But she didn't turn over. We didn't continue that kiss from the dance floor that I had replayed in my mind and felt in my body, which yearned to touch her. I wanted to glide my hands over her breasts, to hear her feel pleasure. I pictured her moaning and a jolt went down my body. As she slept soundly, I struggled silently, my panties twisted in desire. She never slept over again, and I wouldn't feel those sensations arise until the following summer.

AS MY BAND LIFE took a back seat, I leaned into my studies and was accepted into Douglass's acclaimed Institute for Women's Leadership. I was interested in combining art and social justice with media and planned to make a short film for my social action project. This smart group of twelve scholars became a sisterhood. We each came from different backgrounds, cultures, and ethnicities, and through courses, workshops, and guest speakers, we deepened and enriched our conversations on transformational leadership. I loved those connections and discussions. Many professors joined to participate and be part of our world. We were taught public speaking and negotiation by incredible female leaders. My peers planned to go into politics and the field of medicine. It was intimidating and empowering. I was drawn to music, art, and movies. I was drawn to women filmmakers and their stories and perspectives. I saw the opportunity to represent myself and my story and I wanted to experiment with film. It was healing.

By the spring of my junior year, I moved into a dilapidated house on Townsend Street with an amazing group of women, some who were attending college and others who were newly in their careers. They were all passionate, strong-minded, kind, and brave. We had house parties and invited local bands to play in our living room. One day, a housemate ran an entire political campaign from the same spot where we'd hosted a performance the night before. It was a time of independence and growth.

The director of the institute sensed I had insecurities lingering behind my newfound confidence. She saw my ability to step onto the stage and into my power, to channel the limelight from within, but I didn't entirely trust myself. She described me as having lightning in a bottle that was just waiting to be let loose. I could easily feel discouraged and often searched for external affirmation when I could not find it within myself. I was encouraged to follow my interests and signed up for an internship at Women Make Movies located in Manhattan.

Ma was proud when I was accepted into the institute, but when I told her about my interest in media and the organization I'd be interning at, she paused. That's not what she had in mind for me. I watched the expression on her face change. I noticed new wrinkles on her beautiful face. Ma had supported my creative endeavors in the past, but, to her, painting, music, and other creative outlets were hobbies, not a path to a career. She had continued paying for my in-state tuition and covered my rent and all other expenses up until this point. But, even though I was entering the most rigorous time of my college years, she now decided that if I wanted to pursue film and the arts, I would need to get a job and pay for my own rent and bills. I appreciated that this time she gave me a heads-up, but in some ways, the message I internalized was that if I chose myself, I would be on my own. If I followed what my parents wanted, they'd support me. It was conditional.

A friend helped me land a job interview to wait tables at a fancy French restaurant in a well-to-do town between campus and the city. Three nights a week I worked to pay my rent, bills, and cover my weekly round-trip train ticket to Manhattan for my unpaid internship that was about to begin the summer before my senior year. I was excited to explore all that I would learn at my internship and navigate New York City on my own. Each city block was full of characters. The energy the city held was palpable. As if anything was possible, however good or bad.

After a few weeks at my internship, I was flipping through file folders when a woman I had not yet met entered the office. Her walk and posture were the most confident of any woman I had ever seen, and she was dressed in a tailored suit that she absolutely rocked. She had short black hair, wore men's dress shoes, and entered with a flair that mesmerized me. I had never seen a woman dress like that before. It wasn't a costume, nor a classroom assignment. This was her. My mouth was agape this time. Which caught her eye.

"Hi, and who might you be?" she asked.

"I'm... the intern," I managed after a pause, looking down at my shoes.

"I can see that! Welcome. And your name is?" she continued.

"Ingrid," I responded, blushing as I looked back up at her.

"Nice to meet you! I'm Tobi. Hey, would you like a vegan dog?"

I wasn't sure what that was. It sounded gross, but without hesitating, I said, "Sure!"

She left and returned shortly with two vegan hot dogs.

"These are my favorite. What do you think?" she asked.

I took one bite and looked up at her thinking: *Magnificent*.

THE FOLLOWING WEEK, I was asked to type information into a database in the back room as part of my internship duties. I worked with anticipatory excitement as I awaited Tobi's arrival. Each time a staff member walked through the front door, I'd lean over to see if it was Tobi. Finally, the door opened, and it was her. I watched her engage with co-workers and dazzle everyone with her lightheartedness as she made her way to the back room with swagger. I had found out that she was a director and a lawyer who lived on the Upper East Side. She was thirty-six years old. I was twenty-one. She walked right towards me and sat at the desk directly opposite the wall I now stared at. I could feel her energy, which distracted me. Suddenly, it was hard to focus, to type, to do any work. She seemed to feel it, too. At one point, she leaned her head into the doorway and said, "Hi there." Sometime that afternoon we exchanged numbers on a piece of paper that I held with the utmost care. I was infatuated with her. I floated through the city at the end of the day. Boy, did I have a crush on Tobi.

That evening when I got back to my apartment in New Brunswick, I picked up the kitchen landline and carefully opened the piece of paper with her number on it. I was so drawn to her that without hesitating, I rang the number. She picked up.

"Hello?"

I blurted out my confession: how I admired her, that I had never met anyone like her, that I had never felt this way before. She was surprised but enticed by my authentic, romantic approach. She got swept away by my unraveling infatuation. It was so new to me; I couldn't keep it in.

We spoke for three hours that night and she invited me on a date the evening before my next internship shift. I immediately agreed and counted down the days until I'd get to see her. We met in the city and rode the subway up to the Upper East Side. She was confident in the space she held and looked at me in this attentive, sweet, and lusty manner. She started to put her arms around me, but out of nowhere, I froze.

We were getting close to her stop, and I started to notice everyone staring at us in the train car. I suddenly felt outed, different, othered. I wasn't in the safety of an on-campus house party anymore. This was indecent exposure in public. I began to feel the walls cave in, like I had just been shoved in a closet. I was so uncomfortable. It was another spotlight out of my control. It freaked me out.

I tensed up at her advance, recoiling, which was the exact opposite of what I desired to do. My eyes darted around. I was more focused on the onlookers than Tobi. I resisted her touch. I felt like she was making me perform in a dangerous environment. I was far from my comfort zone. She persisted with extreme confidence and ease, which

I wanted to be ready,
to give myself permission
to gallop towards
sexuality like the fierce
person I knew I was.
Instead, fear and shame
swallowed me whole.

seemed to whisper lies—lies that we were, in fact, safe. The train kept going northbound as my heart sank southbound, right into my gut. By the time we arrived at her apartment, I was gutless. I didn't know it at the time, but I was consumed with a boatload of internalized homophobia and fear.

I considered going home, but it was late, and I wasn't familiar enough with Manhattan to navigate all the way back to New Brunswick. *Were trains running at this hour? What if I got stranded? Would anyone from this subway car end up following me?* I let the option of leaving pass. Tobi was a driving force forward, and I followed. But even with that decision made, I couldn't relax or loosen up. I was confused. *What was happening?* I couldn't put any of my experience into words. I was so surprised by how much it consumed me. I went through a bogus evening of attempting to experience physical intimacy with her. She was a woman who knew exactly what she wanted, had a rapture for dirty talk, and was clearly disappointed with the lack of anything pleasurable I could offer her. I could handle kissing but everything else overwhelmed me and I continued to freeze. The next morning, we commuted down to the Lower East Side, agreeing we'd enter the office separately. Walking into my internship that day felt like I had lost a battle. I was completely different.

A few hours into my shift, I got up to pee. The bathroom was outside the main loft door, down a narrow hallway, through a door on the left. There were just a few stalls. I walked towards the mirror. *What is going on with me*, my inquisitive face reflected. The door opened. Tobi had followed me. She turned me towards her in front of the sinks and kissed me passionately. It was sexy and I felt a small spark inside shoot up my spine and leave my knees levitating in the air. I caught a glance of this scene in the mirror. I wanted to be ready for this, to give myself permission to gallop towards sexuality like the fierce person I knew I was. Instead, fear and shame swallowed me whole. Homophobia robbed me of the experience I so deeply craved and yearned for.

As I took the train back to New Brunswick, I slowly went inward, engulfed in defeat. I shrugged at my housemates who supported my big crush feelings, letting them know that the experience hadn't gone well. I couldn't explain how awful it was. For the next few weeks, I hovered on the edge of doubt and indecision. At the last minute, I cancelled a little weekend trip upstate that Tobi had planned for us. She was disappointed with my sheepish reason and didn't understand. How could she? I couldn't communicate with her what I couldn't fully comprehend. I wish I had asked her questions or invited her to share her coming-out story to help me understand what I was experiencing.

This relationship felt like the beginning of a book I wanted to read; instead, I closed it. I shut out her character and the possibility of ever going into that storyline again. I turned my back on being a lesbian and returned to the safety of the make-outs I knew how to handle best—those with boys. I allowed myself to hide, hibernate, away from those scary feelings of infatuation. During office hours with my mentor, the institute director, she asked me how my internship was going. I looked at her and confessed everything—telling her the whole story about Tobi. She sat across from me and listened without judgment. Her expression was one of care. She asked me how I was feeling and reassured me that there was nothing wrong with having a crush on a woman. She encouraged me to be who I was. I loved her for it, but I just wasn't ready.

WHAT I WAS READY FOR was an adventure. An opportunity to spend the rest of the summer in Paris, France, studying art history and architecture came up. I told my parents and was thrilled that not only did they encourage me to register for the experience, they also said they would help fund it.

Having my parents' support meant the world to me. As a family, we had gone to London and Rome in my teen years, but since then, I hadn't returned to Europe. My parents watched me evolve and I felt increasingly seen. We were connecting differently at the dinner table, engaging in conversations about feminism, race, and identity. Once, Ba looked around and remarked he was the only white guy at the table. He laughed about it as I burst into tears. For me, him noticing that he was the only person of privilege at a table of people of color—and laughing about that realization—was shortsighted and othering. It was as if he was unaware of the difficulties we had to experience. I let him know how much race weighed on me and my experience, and that new awareness seemed to stick with him, shifting his perspective.

The conversations at dinner continued. I watched my brother grow out of his punk phase and explore film and screenwriting. He was imaginative and coming out of years of ADHD medication and his own bouts of misunderstanding and objectification. I watched as girls fell for him and attempted to claim him in some way. Ma and Jon had a strong bond, and she couldn't seem to stand any of his friends or girlfriends. No one was good enough—for either of us. She'd refer to our partners and friends as "losers," which made us wonder if she saw us as losers, too.

As Jon continued to discover more of himself and dive into the visual power of storytelling, I packed up for Paris. Ba dropped me off at the airport and I gave him a big hug. It was like he was finally ready to let me go and be an adult on my own terms. Ma had promised to visit me midway through my studies, which I felt excited about. She had been busy with work, so her making a point to visit me in Europe made me feel important.

Before I departed, I was put in touch with another student who'd be on the same flight. We were the last students to arrive in Paris, so it was likely we'd be sharing the last remaining room as roommates. She and I briefly spoke on the phone the night before our flight. She said I could find her by her short black hair. I thought I caught a glimpse of her boarding early when first class was called. She was strikingly unique with red, steel-toed shoes. She *looked* like an artist. I didn't see her anywhere in coach as I made my way to my seat. I wondered, *Is she in first class?* I had scrounged as many points as possible from Ma and Ba's frequent flyer miles to get the first leg of the economy flight to France, paying out of pocket for the return trip. *Who is this girl?*

A few hours into the flight, I decided to get up and find her. I walked past the rows of people sleeping, watching movies, and reading books, and got to the curtains that divided each class. I was about to pull the curtain back to look, when a flight attendant appeared and asked me what I needed. I explained that there was a young woman seated in first class who was attending the same program as I was and had told me to come find her. The attendant gave me a disbelieving look, but when I described the girl who I saw board earlier, they said they'd be back and disappeared behind the curtain. A few moments later, the curtain opened, and there she was staring back at me.

Dane didn't look like anyone I'd ever seen before. She was Portuguese and had caramel skin and killer thick eyebrows. She was edgy. Her voice had a deeper register when she spoke, and she had a big laugh and a sharp wit. At the time, she lived alone in Newark, New Jersey, with a rottweiler that kept her safe. Her family still lived in Portugal, which meant she was often left to her own devices growing up apart from them. We hit it off and chatted for an hour in the area where people stand to stretch or wait for the lavatory. She regaled me with the story of how the flight attendant had come up to find her: "Um, miss, sorry to bother you, but someone from *coach* wants to speak with you."

"How'd you get first class?" I asked. She smiled.

"I had someone who owed me a favor. She hooked me up."

Dane was resourceful, connected, bold. I thought how lucky I was to be on this trip, to meet her.

Dane was the best roommate, and we became immediate friends. In Paris, we attended farmers' markets and picked up roast chickens, potatoes, and tin cans of Portuguese tuna. In the mornings, I'd go down to the patisserie and pick up a baguette. She'd mix the tuna with mayo, add salt and pepper, and make us sandwiches for lunch. The ends of the baguette became an opportunity for dessert, which we used for a Nutella spread. We ate dinner in the hallway of the smallest flat ever as we air-dried hand-washed underwear in our window that opened into a mall. We hung out with the rest of the Rutgers students, studied art for hours, and visited several galleries, museums, and architecturally significant buildings. After a full day of art and studying, we went out on the town and checked out cafés and bars. We talked about traveling to Amsterdam and taking a train to Switzerland on an upcoming weekend. We shared stories about growing up and got to know the other students.

A few weeks later, Ma arrived, and I was happy to welcome her. She was in an energizing mood, sweet and loving to me, and reveled the return to Europe. She was a huge hit with my friends. She and Dane got along well, even though Dane picked up on a few things she felt concerned about—having lost her mother to cancer as a child, she looked out for me. Dane thought my mom had some self-work to do and felt that she placed a heavy weight of expectations on me, however much she was trying to connect.

Throughout the next few days, Ma was generous and cordial, and she seemed content with the experience I was having. On one of her last nights in Paris, all of us students took Ma out to dinner at a nearby café. We spent hours there. Ma was the beloved guest of honor. She was attentive to each of us and offered words of encouragement for our adventure abroad. I watched her sparkle with wisdom. She was truly in her element in that moment. It was beautiful.

Ma left for her next destination, a work trip in Copenhagen, while Dane and I continued our routine of packing lunch every day and studying. We had a lot of papers to write and presentations to prepare for. Dane was expecting her boyfriend to visit. Meanwhile, I blushed each time Ari, one of the girls in our group, flirted with me.

Dane caught one of those interactions, watched my flushed face and shy smile. She and I had talked about girls and our curiosity and attraction to them. Dane had had her own experiences with women back home, even though she was very loyal to her boyfriend. "Ingrid! Go hang out with Ari. She is totally into you!" She was shocked at my quiet resistance.

"I dare you to go down to Ari's apartment," Dane said one night while we were studying in our tiny apartment. I stopped typing my paper abruptly. She egged me on. "Come on, why are you so shy about it?" I didn't tell her about Siouxsie, nor Tobi. I clammed up. But I also felt encouraged by Dane. She was right. *What the hell was I so afraid of?*

I accepted Dane's dare. I knocked on Ari's door. It opened and there she was.

"Hi, Ingrid," Ari whispered, sliding her arm up the door frame, as if she had been waiting for me.

I immediately grew warm and couldn't move. She was so relaxed. I was stiff as a board. She welcomed me into her slightly larger flat that she shared with two roommates, neither of whom were present. She caught my eye as I realized we were alone, and she smiled.

"You know, I've dated girls before," she said provocatively.

She reached for my hand, brought it to her mouth, closed her eyes, and licked it slowly up to the top of my wrist. I could not make sense of what was happening in my body as I contorted with opposing messages. I leaned away and watched her arch her back, as if to remind me of the beautiful set of breasts she had, which I felt drawn to touch and press onto my body. I held on to that possibility for the shortest of seconds before being bulldozed with fear and insecurity. Ari was confident and experienced. She didn't have the same hang-ups I struggled with. I wanted to lean towards her, into this welcomed opportunity to have another go at my desire. I floundered; all my confidence retreated to the confines of my apartment, and I anxiously needed to follow.

"Um, Dane needs me upstairs," I said as I turned to go, leaving her looking bewildered.

"What? No, she doesn't," Ari resisted. She reached up to touch my shoulders and slowly grazed her hands along my arms, then placed her hands in mine. I was crumbling at her touch. She took notice, leaned towards my right ear, and simply whispered, "Well then, have a good night."

I closed my eyes and turned to climb the stairs back to my apartment sheepishly, having let myself forgo another experience that I, and this beautiful girl, wanted.

Understandably, Dane was flabbergasted. "Are you serious?! She did what?! And you're back here?"

I shrugged, deflated by my awkward, defeated response.

"Get back down there!"

I couldn't gather the strength to make another attempt. It was over. What did I know about pleasing a woman? My experience with Tobi made it clear I was bad at it. From my experience with Siouxsie, I worried that nothing would happen again and then I'd be lying in bed awake, feeling like I was going through mild torture. I shuddered thinking about how much I wanted to touch Ari's breasts. I couldn't grant myself permission to touch them. Not quite yet.

WHEN I RETURNED to the States, I was about to enter my senior year—which meant finishing coursework, writing a thesis, and shooting my social action–project film. I kept in touch with Dane, who was starting an all-female art collective called _gaia in Jersey City, which I happily joined. She and I were very close friends, even though we attended classes on different Rutgers campuses, almost thirty miles apart.

For my project, I filmed a series of short vignettes on race, identity, gender, and representation that included my family with my brother at the center, a blonde bombshell exhausted from objectification, a South Asian woman questioning cultural representations as she plays with an Indian Barbie, and a sexualized male who finds solace in housework. I received a small grant for my film and worked with a film student to guide me as I wrote, directed, filmed, and edited the short silent work entitled *A Third Eye Opening*. My parents came to the screening and I couldn't quite read Ma's reaction. It was as if she was processing an abstract concept that she kept to herself. It seemed like an opportunity for her to share her own experiences of racism, sexism, and otherness, but I watched as she kept her arms crossed and shifted her weight in her seat. I focused instead on those who verbalized how they connected with my film and engaged in dialogue. They made me feel seen. Days later, I graduated, ready to take on the world.

Jon's spiked-hair punk stage.

Ma and I during my summer abroad program in Paris.

Dane, my roommate and bestie, in Paris.

六
SWALLOW THE MIC

I GRADUATED WITH A double major in women's and gender studies and art history, and a minor in women's leadership right when the economy and job market took a downturn in 2002. As a new graduate, I applied to all sorts of leadership roles that I believed I was prepared to fill. Several rejections later, I applied to hundreds of entry-level nonprofit and social justice job openings in New York City and received just as many rejections. I was discouraged and felt as though I had fallen from such great heights in my leadership program and training to not be considered for a $10/hour role.

One weekend afternoon, as I shared my woes with Ma in her living room, I started bawling. I crawled into her arms, as she whispered sternly, "Don't let the bastards get you down." I looked up at her calm, encouraging, yet determined expression. She didn't reveal what she was going through as a career-driven female leader. She simply wiped my tears and let me know that I would find work, that this was a difficult time. I just didn't realize that there was more difficulty to come.

A few weeks later, I felt a lump in my breast and told Ma. She helped me get an appointment at a breast clinic. After a series of scans, the physician sat us down and drew a picture of what my cells looked like: a bunch of broccoli florets cramped together, some spread apart from one another. The drawings indicated that two sets of cells were behaving irregularly, which made the physician suspicious. The physician considered a biopsy to determine if the cells were cancerous but then recommended surgically removing both sets of cells to be safe. She said that the surgery would be swift, as would my recovery. That was a relief. I had plans to move to Jersey City by the end of the summer. I had a career to find.

I STARTED TO FEEL a bit loopy as I was wheeled into the surgery room. A person dressed head to toe in white walked over to me, adjusted my hospital gown, and marked the side of my left breast with an X. I could feel my insides, my soul, beginning to panic as my body succumbed to anesthesia. The mark made me feel like my body was slated for a hack job, a cutting, a medical violence. As they moved me to the surgery table, I realized that for the next few hours, my body was in their hands—hands that held a set of tormenting tools.

I woke up post-surgery sore and groggy. I had fractured recollections of floating above my body, looking down at the scene, and screaming at the perpetrators to stop cutting my body. *Stop! Stop! Stop!* Ma was in the waiting room and drove me back to our family home where I planned to rest for a few days. Neither of us thought it would take that entire summer for me to recover.

The surgeon removed several sections of tissue, including the lymph nodes and muscle tissue under my armpit. Thankfully, the tissue was benign. But neither Mom nor I were mentally or emotionally prepared for how much caretaking my healing would require. In the mornings, I was sore and unable to lift my left arm. Ma would wrap her arm around my waist and help me sit up. She'd walk me to the bathroom. I'd slowly take a seat on top of the toilet cover. She'd help remove my top and check my wound.

One morning, she glanced at the wound and back at my face. Seeing the pain I was in, she cried. I looked up and joined her, crying, too. Seeing me in such physical discomfort and needing such care was overwhelming to her. As she looked at my swollen, cut-up left breast, she asked tearily if I wanted reconstructive surgery. I winced. "No more cutting." Surgery was not something I would opt for, but it revealed my mom's openness to cosmetic surgery, which she would secretly pursue in the years to come.

My wound healed following a series of painful scar-tissue injections. It left quite the scar, which made me feel tough. It was a reminder of how unpredictable life is. The way Ma took care of me meant a lot, even if being at home was still uncomfortable. The memories of our family dynamics kept me on edge. At the end of the summer, I decided to rent an apartment in Jersey City with some friends. I was surprised by Ma's reaction. She was upset that I wanted to move out. She wanted me to stay at home. I tried to explain.

"Ma, I need to move and live my life."

Ma didn't express her disappointment with words. It was in her expression and how her posture and body stiffened. I could feel the distance grow between us. I reached out to her as if chasing her fleeting warmth and care. I hugged her, thanking her for taking care of me. She half hugged me back. It was a reminder that if I didn't please her or live up to her expectations, she would punish me by withdrawing, a taste of abandonment and rejection. We had different ideas of how I should live my life. I wondered if there was anything that I wanted that she, too, wished for; or, if she was only ever going to focus on where I fell short. A sadness and guilt tugged at me as I released my arms, questioning myself.

At the same time, it was hard to admit that maybe she was right. Maybe staying home was the smart thing to do for a while. After a month or two in that shared apartment, I still had no job. I was living in a sketchy area of Jersey City and things were going south with my new housemates. I was worried. How could I apply what I learned from the Institute for Women's Leadership if no one would hire me?

Thankfully, one afternoon I received a call from the women's and gender studies department. The leatherbound version of my thesis was available for pickup. The department head explained it had been delayed due to the absence of a department secretary. I quickly responded, "Do you need someone to temporarily help fill that role? I'm available!"

The following week, after an interview and a trial run, I drove back to my college campus where I had graduated just a few months before, to sign a two-year contract. It wasn't the role I was hoping to land after graduation, but I was grateful. The full-time position provided benefits and a salary of $30,000 per year. Ma and Ba were relieved and celebrated that I got a job. Given how close they lived to campus, I'd be able to join them for dinner once a week. Ma smiled with her newly resumed brightness, and I could tell she was reassured and proud.

That my career started as a secretary was a valuable and humbling gift. I didn't immediately see that, especially when former classmates and professors entered the department and were surprised to see me at the desk. I felt embarrassed in those moments but focused on my many tasks. I had received this opportunity, made a commitment, and had the capacity to make improvements in processes, quality, and efficiency, while also providing warmth and camaraderie in the department community. It was like IHOP, but the clientele was a community I knew well.

Another perk of working full-time for the university was tuition remission. I was encouraged by professors to apply to the women's and gender studies MA program. By the time my two-year contract was up, I'd graduate with a master's degree for the cost of books and materials. And so, I applied, was accepted, and retrofitted my life to balance coursework and my nine-to-five. It sucked up every ounce of social life and free time I had, but I knew it was a short-term commitment. During my lunch breaks I read and studied. I commuted to and from Jersey City. When I got back to my apartment, I'd eat dinner and write papers. Twice a week I had class in the evenings and stayed late.

Weekends I read books and wrote more papers. I was just getting into the groove when I met someone on campus who would forever change my life.

Parixit, a petite South Asian skateboarder who loved indie music, played guitar, and was a former Krishna monk, was dead set on starting a band. We were introduced because I had experience being in a college band. He was on the search for a female vocalist. Parixit showed up at my desk from time to time, inviting me out for lunch. He'd tell me to stick around when local shows were going on. One evening, I joined him for an indie concert on campus that featured a female vocalist. Her voice, the band, and the blue light they had choreographed along with their music were all breathtaking. We left feeling inspired.

I wanted to play music, but I hesitated—how would adding music into my world even work? But Parixit reminded me that he, too, worked full-time chipping away at his tuition-free undergraduate degree. He lived with his South Asian family, who were vegetarian and spoke Gujarati. His mom was a stay-at-home parent who made the most incredible Indian food from scratch. I felt welcomed by his family, and seeing Parixit's bicultural experience felt familiar. His parents, too, allowed him to turn their garage into a band rehearsal space.

Parixit introduced me to Vasilios—who went by "Vasil"—a kind, tall, and muscular Greek guy who had founded his own indie record label. After months of scheduling conflicts, we finally arranged a jam session. That night after work, Parixit and I entered Vasil's basement studio, which was filled with an amazing setup of synths and instruments.

It was like an underground world that I was completely enamored by. Drawn to one of his synths, I sat down and played until I found a sequence that I couldn't stop repeating. It flowed through me. I forgot that Vasil and Parixit were behind me. But it was as if we were all in the same trance, entering the same vortex together. Parixit started playing guitar and Vasil created a bass riff on another synth. Vocals began to pour out of me, as if no time had passed since the last time I sang into a mic.

That night, the three of us wrote what would become "Waves and Generation," the first song on our debut album *Lines of Parallel Minds*, which would soon be signed by Cult Hero Records.

THE 303S, the name of that very first synth I played at Vasil's studio, became my first official band. We played shows, released an album, had articles written about us, and went on tour. Parixit and I were the main songwriters. We loved the music we made together, and our creative process was deeply special. We could play and riff, build and communicate through the music, to the degree where talking became more difficult. We were both so busy with school and full-time work that adding weekly band practices and weekend recordings to the mix led to a lot of exhaustion and pressure. An influx of musicians, mostly drummers and bassists, filled out the rest of the band. Parixit became a second brother to me, and we'd hash things out like blood relatives do.

The music we wrote was magical—like we were communicating with the great beyond. When I look back at the lyrics we wrote, they speak even more to me at present—especially when it comes to experiences I would have decades later. Parixit took the band very seriously. Sometimes I mistook that for egotism and thought he was making it all about him. But that wasn't the case. He had a heart condition that he kept quiet about. His doctors had said he might not live beyond the age of thirty. He was determined to express himself through music; he was racing against an internal ticking clock, which made his drive intense.

Even when we bickered, music was the way towards understanding. We'd both be in disbelief that separate recording sessions could yield an output that was unified and clear, filled with empathy and understanding. We grew more confident in our ability to play instruments, how to deal with unforeseen technical difficulties when playing live—which had me in tears—and experiment with different instruments. We went from being a bit intimidated by the stage to thrashing across it like we were in the privacy of our living rooms. I'll never forget a show we played in Jersey City. All these young fans were singing along to our songs. They *knew* the lyrics! It was an incredible experience—I laughed when I got a word or phrase wrong and the audience corrected me.

Being close in proximity to other mixed-race and culturally mixed friends and musicians brought up deep conversations about identity, which in turn inspired songs. Parixit and I wrote about social pressures and the tension of strained relationships with lovers or parents, and we talked openly about sexuality and expectations. Being outsiders, in between, half in and half out, Parixit and I connected through music. We encouraged each other not to feel confined or defined by labels. Something deep inside me was coming to the surface, and it was beautiful.

AS I WRAPPED my final semester of graduate school and my two-year work contract, I had one thing left to do to graduate: select a summer practicum—a six-week, on-the-ground experience that would culminate in writing yet another thesis. I was curious about the statistical drop in preteen girls' self-esteem and wanted to experiment with what might combat that, address their needs, remove the mean-girl culture, and create an experience that would draw on their collective power, resistance, and rebellion—a.k.a. confidence. As I was running out of time and options, a friend mentioned a rock 'n' roll camp happening in the Northwest. *Thank you, universe.*

In 2001, the Rock 'n' Roll Camp for Girls launched in Portland, Oregon, drawing hundreds of girls aged eight to eighteen to apply. Just as many female musicians signed up as band coaches, mentors, and performers. These weeklong sessions offered 50 percent of the attendees financial aid scholarships.

In 2004, I reached out to the founder who welcomed me to join the camp's summer programs. I packed up my belongings and flew to Portland. I had never been to the Northwest before. I answered a Craigslist ad to sublet someone's room while they were out of town. The timing was perfect, and the apartment was located biking distance from the camp. The camp founder picked me up from the

Our call to action was to always represent yourself and who you are—*your* identity. None of us fit in molds.

airport, but as we pulled up to the address of the apartment, we saw a bunch of punk kids sitting on the stoop. She looked at the house and asked, "You sure this is it?" I checked the address again on the piece of paper I carried with me. It was correct.

"I'll wait out here, go check it out," she said. I hesitated, then got out of her van, grabbed my belongings, and walked up towards the punk kids. They nodded when I explained whose room I was renting and one of them showed me the way. I was alarmed by the state of the apartment. It was cold, dirty, and when I entered the room there was a mattress on four cinder blocks. No sheets, towels, or blankets. It was a real shithole.

To say I felt homesick and scared is an understatement. The camp founder offered to let me crash with her and her girlfriend that night. The next day she gave me a set of sheets, towels, and a loaner bike so I could return to the dilapidated apartment. I was so thankful, and she reminded me that I was offering my services all summer for free. What I didn't realize is how much the camp would give back to me tenfold.

One week before the first camp session launched, I reviewed the applications of admitted attendees with another mixed-race staff member, and we realized that 30 percent identified as multicultural and of two or more races. We considered the opportunity here. What if we created a workshop that explored identity in a way that was relatable to eight- to eighteen-year-olds? We worked together to come up with a creative approach that provided language for how to talk about sexism, racism, and otherness—language we hadn't grown up with—and content that explained the purpose and impact of media portrayals of women and girls. Our call to action was to always represent yourself and who you are—*your* identity. None of us fit in molds.

We spent the remaining days and evenings creating a curriculum. We wanted to make sure the workshop combined a depth and simplicity that would be meaningful across the broad range of ages. We knew that our workshop was experimental and groundbreaking. Once camp started, we were given the green light to launch and co-facilitate this new workshop, which we coined "Image Versus Identity." My co-facilitator and I ran our workshop three times, and it was well received. After one session, an eight-year-old came up to me and said, "Thank you for teaching us about gender dichotomies!" It was electrifying. That workshop would eventually expand globally to more than fifty rock 'n' roll camps for girls, something we never imagined.

THAT FIRST WEEK at Rock 'n' Roll Camp was the most empowering experience I've ever had with other women. I had never been around so many female musicians and queer women before. The sisterhood, kindness, acceptance, and community were a welcome outpouring after the drought of sustained female connection in my youth.

Every female mentor taught music—bass, guitar, keys, vocals, and drums—and coached girls on how to work together to come up with original songs that they'd perform on stage by the end of the week. Other activities included attending workshops about the history of women in rock, watching mentors' bands perform—which was exhilarating and inspiring—and ending each day with positive affirmations and a dance party.

One mentor taught a workshop on self-defense. I had to run out the door and gasp for air after half of the teen girls shared their experiences of sexual abuse and rape. It was so deeply painful. For many, it was the first time they had ever told anyone about what they'd experienced. The safe space camp generated was full of respect, care, recognition, and friendship. Camp was a unique bubble that left the socially constrictive dynamics of gender, identity, and other norms outside. Girls who entered with low self-esteem became powerful onstage and glued to the mic. They felt heard, their voices encouraged and newly amplified among new, supportive peers and mentors. We taught them to see the mic as a tool, to get so close that they could almost swallow it. Nothing else in their lives—or in our lives as mentors—offered an experience like rock camp.

On the Saturday that concluded camp, each new band performed their song at a local venue with the entire camp community and their families cheering them on. Guiding a newly formed band to write a song together was one thing, but being their trusted cheerleader and conductor at the base of the stage, encouraging them through every second, was even more joyful. I witnessed the buildup of doubt before each performance. I saw that in my own experience as a young musician. But having camp friends and mentors cheering you at the front of the stage pushed doubt and pressure of perfection out of the way. It might have been the highlight of their young lives. At camp, you learned the truth and what really matters in a trusting and caring environment. And in that love, rebellion, and dynamic of coaching and learning, we witnessed transformation. Years later when I managed teams, I'd be asked by other leaders why I took on such a cheerleading approach. No matter our age, as adults we're still young kids onstage, performing. Our careers, our lives, can feel like a performance, one with fear, doubt, and insecurity. We can even feel like we're acting a part or role in a play. Having a coach enter that space without judgment—to explore, to encourage, to question—can spark opportunities for possibility, unlearning, truth, and getting our confidence, voice, and power back. And all that can happen within a short span if we're immersed in that experience and feel it in a deep, groundbreaking way. I learned that at camp.

Watching the girls at rock camp transform throughout the week had a major effect on all of us mentors and volunteers. It gave us hope for a different reality than we experienced as women and girls. Being there was a way to give the next generation what we never had and revel in it, together. Rock camp was an oasis. The catharsis I felt was compounded by all that I witnessed, as if catharsis was rippling throughout the space and you could see it. At camp, I was part of a sisterhood of female rock musicians. Gender was bendy, and everyone was brave in their identity, self-expression, and sexuality. We were all different and accepted. I loved this queer community and felt extremely seen on a deep level.

I had a boyfriend at the time, and what's funny is that each time I mentioned him during the back-to-back weeklong sessions, every volunteer was so surprised. They'd say,

"But you are *so* gay! You love boobs!" They weren't wrong about my fascination with boobs, but again, I *had* a boyfriend. Each time this conversation occurred someone would place a comforting arm around me as if to say: *You're so gay, dude, but sure, take your time.*

One of the volunteers—a bassist from an all-girl band based in Brazil—and I had a routine of downing loads of free coffee in the morning and then talking about our aching stomachs when the caffeine hit too hard. She was androgynous with short hair, a nose ring, and tattoos. She spoke broken English and always made me laugh. After the third and final weeklong session of camp, there was a volunteer wrap-up party. I asked for her address so that I could write her letters and keep in touch. I wasn't sure if it was the loud music or my prudish question, but something got lost in translation.

"You want a kiss?" she asked.

Surprised, I was about to respond but she beat me to it.

"Sure, not a problem," she answered. And before I knew it, her soft lips were on mine as she kissed me gently, and I felt the metal of her lip ring graze my mouth, as if drawing a picture of this moment. My knees buckled underneath me, but I was still standing. It was as if time slowed down, and we were making out in slow motion. I was carried away by the sensations radiating through me, as if the instinct I had forced to go dormant inside me was reignited. As our lips parted, she smiled and said, "Okay, bye!" and off she went, as the shock wave of awareness kept rippling through me. I floated back to my shithole apartment and into my room, as the punk kids blasted music through the paper-thin walls. I had already packed for my flight home and was going to head to the airport in a few hours. I couldn't sleep. I kept fantasizing that she'd show up and we'd make out and throw ourselves onto the mattress held up by cinder blocks. I never wanted someone so badly.

THE NEXT DAY, my boyfriend—my last attempt to make a straight relationship work—picked me up at the airport in New York City. We had a dinner date in Connecticut that evening to see friends who were in a band together and had just had a baby. I was tired but obliged, despite feeling totally out of place. I wanted to talk about the kiss and what happened, but I was sidelined by a classic display of heteronormativity.

My boyfriend seemed genuinely eager to replicate the two-musicians-who-marry-and-make-a-baby scenario. I felt a tightness in my throat. That life just wasn't for me. I was tired of trying so hard to make this work. The signs were telling me that my sexuality was wrestling with my homophobia, and it was gaining the upper hand. And after that kiss, it was too clear to ignore.

On the drive home as I watched the city outside the car window, I worked up the courage to speak my truth. For both our sakes. I loved this man, but I couldn't choose him over me without eventually resenting him and possibly hating myself. I had learned at camp to watch out for the times you make yourself small, invisible, accommodating for others. And in that moment, I felt small and contained. I sat on my hands, which were starting to shake, and took a deep breath. *I am a brave warrior.*

No matter our age, as adults we're still young kids onstage, performing.

"I unexpectedly kissed a girl last night. And . . . I . . . think I need to explore these feelings. I think . . . that I . . . like girls."

It wasn't the first time we had talked about girls, or what he framed as issues between me and my mother and my father. In his silence now, I felt an immediate distance build up between us. It felt like an eternity went by, though we had gone just a few short blocks. Finally, his obviously pained, yet cruel, response: "It's not my fault you're dumb."

That hurt and stung. I was *not* dumb. Kissing girls was not dumb. Liking girls was not dumb. I was sharing my truth, which was out of *love*. And now, feeling rejected and misunderstood, I silently raged. By the time we parked, I was seething. Neither of us had spoken again after his comment. I marched into his apartment, gathered my things, and left. I headed back to the apartment in Jersey City I had rented with fellow musicians on the same record label. As I drove from Brooklyn across Manhattan, I realized I had chosen myself. Walking through my apartment door, I announced to my housemates that I had finally, evidently, come out. They looked at me and said: "Yep, about time! *You're so gay, dude.*"

AFTER SUBMITTING my thesis, "I Want to Rock Out: On Acting vs. Appearing at the Rock 'n' Roll Camp for Girls," I graduated with an MA in women's and gender studies. My mom, dad, and brother came to my graduation and applauded me. Ma was skeptical about my degree and what I could do with it. But we didn't have much opportunity to debate. Soon after, the 303s went on tour with our labelmates Lismore in Canada. I did double duty on the tour as

Lismore had lost their bass player, and I offered to fill in. I quickly learned how to play bass and loved it. Music and the stage were becoming a part of my life.

After our short tour, I began teaching a gender studies course for a term as an adjunct professor and consulting for a foundation, thanks to connections I made in graduate school. I was getting coffee with a friend on campus when she introduced me to a stunning woman named Dee. Dee had green eyes and wore thick black eyeliner that made them pop. She was gorgeous, tall, and edgy, wearing a motorcycle jacket and Chuck Taylors. Half her head was dyed black, and the other half bleached blonde. She was a mix of flirtatious and goofy. I found her charming. Before I left the café, she handed me a piece of paper with her email address and smiled at me. I never blushed so hard.

Email exchanges led to phone calls. Phone calls led to a date. We met at a bar in Jersey City and within minutes, she leaned in towards my face and we started making out. It felt amazing, until that pang in the back of my neck reminded me that people were looking at us. She pulled me closer, as if she could feel my reaction, and put her hands on my waist, holding me steady. Alarm signals were going off in my brain and I started backing off. In response, she leaned in with confidence.

"Never mind who's looking, who cares what they think? Right now, I am kissing you and you're kissing me. And I don't want to stop."

She was convincing and challenged me to confront my fear and shame. It was melting away and gushing like water released from a dam. We made out at the bar, even groped one another, and then headed back to my apartment. We explored our bodies and ways to pleasure one another. It was like nothing I had ever experienced. My fear of being a terrible lesbian lover was leaving front stage, yet I kept looking for the exit doors. New can be scary.

Dee was fluid with her sexuality and helped me feel less insecure with myself and being with a woman. As I grew more confident, it felt like I had a lot of catching up to do. I was coming out on a fast track at last. I felt like a teenager—there was an element of danger, of being found out, but it felt right. Her boldness reminded me of my own. Her love encouraged me to give love back to myself. Her smile and her moans turned every fiber in my body on high. I had such a mix of dopamine and oxytocin those several months that we were together. Through rebellion, I found connection to myself, and to women. The whole world was my gay oyster. She and I went to queer parties and I dove headfirst into this aspect of my identity. *I was all in.*

ALTHOUGH NO ONE in my friend group seemed surprised when I came out, the fact that I hadn't yet told my parents loomed in my mind. My brother knew, and he was incredibly supportive. Ba had an idea, and I knew he'd be much easier to tell than Ma. Both my parents had met Dee, who was now my girlfriend, but they kept referring to her as "your friend." I didn't feel comfortable explaining or contradicting them.

One night, Dee joined me for dinner at my parents' house. Dinner turned into dessert, and Ba was eager to put an old film on, which brought us well into the evening. My parents urged us to sleep over in my old bedroom, where I had recovered from surgery just a few summers before. Dee and I looked at each other and agreed, said good night, and crawled into bed in our street clothes. I felt the same comfort I'd felt years before when KC slept over and spooned me after telling me she was bisexual. And here I was, spooning my girlfriend. How far I had come! I put my arm around Dee and, though it felt odd being in my parents' house, I let my happiness and her warmth lull me to sleep.

In the morning, I woke up startled. Ma had barged in—there were still no boundaries at my parents' house—and she abruptly took my arm off Dee's fully clothed waist. No words were spoken. In hindsight, I could have asked Ma what was going on in her mind. What was her fear? What was she trying to protect me from? Instead, Ma made some remark about how you're not supposed to touch your friends—almost as if she was recollecting something she had been told.

On the drive back to Jersey City, Dee looked at me and said she understood. She'd had her own difficulties with her parents. She gave me space and didn't add any pressure but made herself available if I wanted to talk about it. At the age of twenty-five, I finally reached this destination in my life. I wanted my family to know and be a part of this important aspect of my identity. I decided it was time to come out to Ma.

The next afternoon, I took a deep breath and called her. As the phone rang, I wondered what she was doing, if she was in the middle of something, if the call would just go to voicemail. My hands were starting to feel sweaty. Was I

She was on one side of
the riverbank and everything
that kept us apart—
religion, language, culture,
race, and now my sexuality—
kept widening the
distance between us.

going to have this conversation over the phone? I became nervous and was second-guessing myself. I considered hanging up, but the call connected, and I heard my mom's voice.

"Wei? Ing-ga."

"Hey Ma, I, I... have to tell you something," I said with determination and concern in my tone.

The other end of the line went very quiet. This was unusual for Ma, who we often joked held the talking stick in most conversations.

Finally, she responded with "Oh?" as if bracing herself.

I took a breath.

"I want to tell you that Dee... she isn't just a friend... she is my—"

"Do not continue," Ma abruptly interrupted. "Think about what you're going to say. Because if it is what I think you're going to say, you should know that you will be disowned from the family."

Now it was my turn to go quiet. *Is she serious?*

"Disowned from the family?" I repeated, in disbelief. "Ma, I'm a grown woman. You can't mean that!"

"Yes, I do mean that." Another pause. "Goodbye." Click, she hung up.

I held on to the phone receiver. I looked down at the phone in shock, yet my eyes could see in such clarity the contours of the buttons on the phone, the symmetry of the cord, the invention itself.

I slowly put down the receiver and shed a tear. It was like there was always a river between us. She was on one side of the riverbank and everything that kept us apart—religion, language, culture, race, and now my sexuality—kept widening the distance between us. As I sat alone, feeling her rejection and the threat of true abandonment, I pictured how far apart those riverbanks had become. There was a roaring tide between us as we stood on our respective cliffs. Even if I were to shout across the distance, she couldn't hear me. It seemed I had no way to reach her.

top Three generations of warrior spirits: Me, Ma, and Nai Nai.

bottom Jon and I during our year of living together.

Out and about in Taipei with Nai Nai.

七

RAGE AGAINST THE STAGE

WHEN I TURNED twenty-six, I became a founding member of the Willie Mae Rock Camp for Girls based in Brooklyn. I felt similar magic happen in this newly formed experience. I was welcomed and embraced, which is what I needed after realizing I might not have that with my family. I helped with media coverage, fundraised, and performed at events. I found sponsors and spread the word. And as usual, camp gave back. I met several queer musicians, one of whom needed a guitarist for a thirty-three-day tour across the US that upcoming fall.

Boyskout was a lesbian-oriented band that made sexy music videos. I was intrigued that they were all female, which I had never experienced in a band before. But how would I manage being in a *third* band in addition to the 303s and Lismore? I considered how the 303s were starting to fracture. Parixit's intensity and my focus on my newfound identity were at odds. I couldn't help but home in on this aspect of my life and give it my full attention. I wanted to experience playing music with women who shared my sexuality. I needed community and support, and distance from home.

The timing of the tour seemed right for a few reasons. Dee was moving to San Francisco to start a graduate program. We were uncertain about a long-distance relationship, and a tour was a welcomed distraction for the pang of what was coming: my first breakup with a woman I cared for and loved. Plus, I was between jobs. I had just wrapped up my consulting and teaching gigs and received a full-time job offer in New York City at the Academy for Educational Development. The role included capturing trends in media-based after-school programs, like my work at rock camp, which was expanding globally. I had an advisory board, a major funder, and creative runway. I would commute from Jersey City to my office on Fifth Avenue and I was eager to begin. I negotiated a start date for when I returned from tour and felt relieved I had that secured.

First, I needed to learn Boyskout's songs on guitar. Their riffs were more challenging than my current skillset afforded. I flew to the South by Southwest music festival (SXSW) to watch them perform and get to know the members. My friend, the singer and lead guitarist, was ecstatic and introduced me to her motley crew. But the vibe wasn't the same as with the mentors and volunteers at rock camp. Some members seemed a bit unhinged. We all crammed into one hotel room booked for the night. The guitarist I was to replace flirtatiously tried to get in my pants as I was sandwiched between her bandmates in a queen bed. On the second bed, another band member was quietly instigating foreplay with a male groupie on the bed next to us, telling him to shut up any time he made a sound. I looked over at her. Wasn't she aware we weren't yet asleep? Two other people slept on the floor. As I flew home the next morning, I wondered if that was atypical or the norm. *Who were these girls?* I had made a commitment so I continued learning their songs and prepared for the tour, which would begin in two weeks' time in San Francisco. I had no idea what I was getting myself into, even though all the signs were laid out clear as day in front of me.

I flew to San Francisco for a weekend of band practices before the tour took off. It was grueling and exhausting, but I managed to play well enough. Two girls appeared to have a drinking problem, and one made it clear she didn't think my guitar playing was up to snuff. On the last night, I finally played well enough for her to agree that we were ready to perform. The next morning, we packed up the fifteen-passenger van with our instruments, amps, drum kit, and our individual small sacks of personal belongings.

That thirty-three-day tour taught me so much about patience and resilience: how to communicate with people who were unstable; how to read people and navigate interactions with strangers; and how to manage long hours behind the wheel. It was always such a blessing to make a pit stop and exit the van to stretch, breathe fresh air, and look around at the small-town surroundings.

At some of these stops, locals sat on lawn chairs and stared at us disapprovingly. *Who brought in the city riffraff?* they seemed to say. Seeing us was a surprise to some and improper, even shocking to others. Yet at shows, the audience loved us. Girls showed up to our shows in each city, dancing and cheering. It was a radical experience. As a newly out lesbian, I loved being onstage with fellow queers. Being in this queer, all-female spotlight onstage—out, confidently playing guitar, and presenting my own take on androgyny and sexuality—was awesome and reassuring. Yet one night, the spotlight reintroduced the same kind of image and objectification I had once taught girls to avoid at rock camp.

We were playing one of our last songs, when unannounced, the female promoter hopped on the stage. She came right up to me as I was playing guitar and without pausing, wrapped her hand around the back of my head and pushed her mouth against mine—a nonconsensual French kiss. The crowd cheered but I felt startled by her lack of boundaries and treatment of me like I was a sex object—a character to behold. I didn't want to be a character. I didn't want to be seen through the desire of onlookers. It felt like the spotlight enhanced my otherness and sexuality as an open invitation. Whatever wall that separated the stage and performers from the audience and crowd was now breached.

My bandmates smiled as if they thought it was cool. Attention was good for the band. But it wasn't what I wanted. I reflected on what had happened earlier in the tour. We had crashed at someone's house to save money. Through the floor vent, I overheard two of the female hosts arguing about who would get to have *sex with me*. I was horrified and clung tightly to my sleeping bag. I looked at the door to make sure that it was in fact locked. I stayed up anxiously wondering how to shut their fantasy down if they came barging in. It was as if they pictured me waiting, ready to receive and welcome advances from either of them. This part of the gig I hadn't signed up for.

It was a conflicting experience. On the one hand, I was a confident female musician who felt the stage was my home away from home. On the other, I was losing control of how I wanted to be seen. I didn't want to be objectified, and my image was distorted in this light. I even fought off other touring musicians we played with, their roadies, and fans. I wanted to be seen, respected, and valued as a human being. Yet the media wasn't helping. We did a shoot for *Curve* magazine and got the cover—with the title "Sexiest Women in Rock." I wish they could have come up with a more interesting approach, rather than focusing on our appearance. But image has currency.

That night, after the promoter make-out fiasco, I kept to myself and packed up my gear. We had made it to the East Coast, and I was eager to get to my aunt's house that evening. She lived close to Baltimore, Maryland, where we had just played, and offered to host us. Aunt Janet, my dad's sister, was supportive and accepting, and enjoyed watching my journey as a musician. She was even more excited when we arrived with blunts, which was a gift from a fan. I was so relieved and happy to connect with my aunt, someone who really knew and loved me. I immediately relaxed in her home. It was a familiar, familial environment, and I basked in the opportunity to sleep by myself in her guest bedroom. It was one of the few times I slept alone during that tour and felt 100-percent safe.

Perpetually underslept and tired, we left after lunch to make it to sound check at a venue in Philadelphia. That evening's show was a blur. I had my sights fixed on getting to my parents' house in central New Jersey and reuniting with my Lismore bandmates who were joining Boyskout onstage.

As we drove up another major highway, we first had to play a live radio gig in northern Jersey, which Ba came to with his college friend. They leaned on the wall and chatted as they watched us perform. Ba was proud. His daughter was a touring rock musician. He knew I was gay, and he was supportive under Ma's radar. Ma hadn't brought up our painful phone conversation. The few times we saw one another before I left for tour she ignored it as if it had never happened. I couldn't be a gay daughter. And so, to her, I wasn't. I knew that she thought I was promiscuous and that this was all a phase. Ma would liken me to a light that moths were drawn to, only to end up scattered on the ground in the morning. I wasn't surprised at this, since she also said things like "to be a woman, you must cut your own wings." It was a polarizing period in our mother-daughter relationship. And yet, our experiences as women couldn't be more similar.

The pressures of identity and objectification were yet again weighing me down and holding me back from taking flight. I did feel like women flew to me like moths to a flame, as I did to them. But whether we ended up on the ground or cut our own wings, that was external and societal harm. Ma and I had spaces we occupied where we felt confident and could express ourselves, but like all women, and particularly women of color, we were reminded about the social containers we were stacked within.

Ma didn't come to the live radio gig; she stayed behind to cook for the pack of hungry bandmates that would soon accompany me at home. I was looking forward to seeing her, awaiting the taste of her home cooking, and eager to sleep in another bed all to myself. When we finished the radio gig and packed up the van, Ba offered me a ride back home. The van could follow. That separation was welcomed.

On the drive home, Ba wanted to hear about the tour. He let me know that he and Ma were thinking of how best they could support me should my music career take off. *My music career?* I felt moved. My parents were trying to understand and see me, accept a possibility that was beyond their cultural norms, separate from their own expectations. It was different. I assured Ba: "I'm learning a lot, it's an adventure for sure, but this isn't a career for me." When we arrived, I hugged Ma. Her embrace was brief as she went into hosting mode, ignoring how boyish and gay her guests appeared. Instead, she focused on my new job and the speaking engagements and leadership experiences to come after the tour wrapped.

Somewhere in my gut I knew that Ma and I were aligned on what a career meant for the both of us and what the stage would become. Although music and performing would still be in my near future, the dynamic between me and the spotlight was going to change.

AFTER A WILD ENDING to our tour that took us west again, I flew back east to start my new job. I found a new two-bedroom apartment in Jersey City that, in a surprising turn of events, my brother and I moved into. My parents would pay half the rent to cover his portion, and he moved into what really was more of an office than a second bedroom. Jon was now studying film studies at Hunter College. That year I got to watch him become more independent. He wrote descriptive, beautifully written screenplays and he was also a musician—he was a much better guitarist than me, as I preferred playing bass and synth.

Our apartment had a large, open space as you entered, which was often turned into a stage for performances, band practices, and once, the set of a music video. We wheeled our laundry to the corner laundromat and found furniture on Craigslist ads. We commuted to our respective Manhattan-based subway stops. On Sundays, we cleaned the apartment and made dinner together. Often, I'd come home from work to my brother playing electric guitar on one of our amps.

Always a looker, Jon had no problem attracting women. I often felt protective of him as he, too, was pursued and desired for his unique appeal, killer jawline, and handsome mixedness. But in our apartment, it was just the two of us in our hapa sibling oasis. We cooked Chinese food together and hosted parties. I look back at that year living with my brother fondly, even if it must have been eye-opening to him how involved I was with bands and my queer social life. It was vibrant, connective, and alive.

At the end of the year, the landlord didn't renew our lease. Jon and I decided to move separately to Brooklyn—he, secretly, with his girlfriend, unbeknownst to our parents, and me, to Williamsburg where Boyskout had moved and most of the girl parties were thrown. It was a time of experimentation, learning, and growing.

I did increasingly well at my job. I hired my first direct report and got promoted to editor-in-chief of *Youth Media Reporter*. I was invited to be a keynote speaker in Maastricht in the Netherlands to talk about the youth media movement happening in the US. I invited Ma to join me on my trip to Europe and, to my delight, she agreed.

Traveling with Ma was a special mother-daughter treat. I had grown up a lot since her Paris visit. And I had learned how to engage with an audience onstage and now, about topics that I cared about, like social justice, representation, and the voices of the next generation. I enjoyed creating learning experiences, workshops, and programs for young people that spurred them to think outside the box, to question social constructs, and to share what made them each unique. Ma loved this version of who I was becoming. She had a framed photo of me at the podium on her desk.

We first flew to Brussels, where I took her to a flea market. I loved finding local flea markets and garage sales growing up and during my days on tour. Ma never quite understood my interest in searching for treasure at secondhand shops, thrift stores, and yard sales, or my magnetic pull to flea markets. The first time we went to a secondhand store in New Jersey together, she started off uninterested and even slightly annoyed until she, too, found a treasure in the sea of junk.

After the flea market, we walked through the streets and explored. We came across a crêperie, Ma's favorite, but another scent caught her attention. We looked across the street and saw a vendor selling Belgian-chocolate waffles. We exchanged glances and, in silent agreement, sped to the

It was as if the gold
I was becoming could
be tossed into the
well's depths, covered
in grit and grime,
lost without its shine.

cart to place an order for two. As we ate the delicious treat, we scanned the area for a place to have dinner that evening. We landed on—of all places—a Japanese hibachi restaurant. It was such a great way to explore the city together, finding unexpected gems along the journey all by happenstance. We relished the experience.

During our dinner, Ma told me about a Chinese idiom about having to go through fire multiple times to become pure gold. She explained how every hardship we experience helps purify us, deepening us at our core. For her, this reflected her spirituality and religious beliefs. For me, it was about bravery and wisdom. The idiom reminded me of my warrior great-grandmother, my commanding nai nai, my incredible ma, and me. Each of us took big leaps in life, towards what we believed in or felt was right. For me, it was about living my truth. Ma hadn't accepted my truth—that I was queer. I wasn't the straight woman she wanted me to be. I wondered how many rounds of fire it would take for her to see my authentic self as pure gold.

The morning of my keynote talk in Maastricht, I was suddenly nervous. I didn't feel prepared. Ma helped me. She listened to me practice the introduction and made sure I had a printed copy with me just in case I needed to refer to my notes. The event was packed. I saw Ma take a seat in the middle aisle of the audience. I walked out to the podium, took a breath, and began. I could see Ma smile, seeing my potential. That was, until I started playing short media clips that young people in New York City had made.

Each clip was about identity and representation and the final clip was about sexuality. I caught Ma's expression, which had changed to horror and embarrassment. I had embarrassed my mom. In front of everyone. My heart sank. I finished the keynote and smiled through the applause. I gathered my things as people got up for a coffee break. Ma sat still in her chair. I walked up to her.

"So... Ma, what did you think?" I asked, quietly.

Her concerned expression was unchanged. "I don't think you should have shown that video. The topic wasn't relevant," she said bluntly.

"Ma, it couldn't be more relevant. These are stories young people are sharing about their lives, through media production. That's what the conference is about."

"Yes, but not *that* topic."

Somewhere in the back of my mind, I knew she had enjoyed the trip and seeing me speak. It was a version of the spotlight that felt right to me. But Ma's doubts could easily push me to the bottom of a what felt like a well. And in that well, I questioned my worth and my value. It took several days before I could climb out of the mental well and reaffirm that maybe I was enough. I knew who I was and that I had guts, but the power of her shame and its imprint on me was profound. It was as if the gold I was becoming could be tossed into the well's depths, covered in grit and grime, lost without its shine.

MY CAREER provided stage opportunities, but I was still interested in playing music and performing. The sun had set on my roles in the 303s, Lismore, and Boyskout. But then I met Sarah.

Like Parixit, Sarah wanted to jam. She was persistent about it and eventually we borrowed the studio that Boyskout occupied. And thank goodness we did. With Sarah on drums, I played bass and synth, and sang. A magical flow of music took over. Like how the 303s came to be, that night Sarah and I wrote our first song, "Foxy," birthing our dance duo, Rad Pony.

Sarah and I both took our careers seriously. She was a Yale-graduate architect who had started her own company. She had a Valley-girl accent even though she grew up on the East Coast. She made me laugh! She knew she was queer most of her life. In college, she joined a sorority to meet girls. I was flabbergasted.

"I don't think that's why women join sororities, Pony." I chuckled.

Sassily, she answered, "Well, that's why *I* joined!"

We were bandmates, best friends, soul sisters, and what we coined "pony sisters." She was in a long-term, serious relationship with Holly, who also happened to be mixed-Asian, whom I connected with and cared for. Sarah and Holly met at Yale. Holly was a lawyer who helped women in the legal system. Their love and commitment had a major impact on me. I realized, through watching them, that my desired future was a harmonious life spent side by side with a woman I loved.

Sarah and I recorded two albums as Rad Pony. We had a few tours on both coasts and played a handful of festivals. We were never signed, as that wasn't our goal. We drew a fun, queer-friendly crowd that liked to dance. We played with costumery and showed a more feminine side. We welcomed guest musicians and collaborated with artists. Balancing our band with full-time jobs felt manageable, and it stayed that way for two fantastic years.

And then the 2008 recession hit. And it hit my parents the hardest. Ma, despite her success as a tech pioneer in mobility, had been laid off after a merger with Google. Her executive role was replaced by three employees.

Ba had run a successful company that went out of business suddenly. During this time, whenever I visited home, I would pay for my parents' groceries. At the checkout counter, I'd offer to pay, and Ba would defeatedly say, "I'm in no position to refuse." My heart broke. A seed of financial insecurity and fear made its way into my brain.

My parents had no other option but to put their dream home up for sale. It was part of their retirement plan, and that, too, was drastically changing. Jon, who now worked in Manhattan, came down to join me at our parents' house to help them shed their belongings. They had a buyer for the house, thankfully, and needed help downsizing. We organized a weekend-long garage sale. I remember seeing Ma's face red with exhaustion as she tried to go through items, rapidly recalling their memories and having to choose what to keep and what to part with. All her beautiful houseplants were too large to bring with her and I could see the toll it took on her face. Her sanctuary would need to be rebuilt.

That weekend, we watched 75 percent of my parents' furniture and belongings get swooped up for lowball deals in an everything-must-go sale. Possessions were parted with; plants that weren't sold were cut up and composted. It would take years for my parents to feel the freedom that comes with shedding one's belongings. But, for now, my parents were safe. They rented a condo, resituated to their new home life, and adapted. That major life change opened the possibility for more to come.

THE RECESSION caught up to my job, and after four years in my role, I needed to begin another job hunt in a difficult and competitive job market. It was déjà vu, reminding me of the intense job search after the 2001 crash. Finally, after a year and a half of job hunting and interviewing while stretching the funds from my position at the Academy, I got an offer for a director role at a nonprofit. The role was in line with my career trajectory—but there was just one problem. It was based in San Francisco. I had a big decision to make.

I spoke with my family about it. On the one hand, Ma didn't like the idea of me being so far away, and Jon and Ba agreed. On the other, this was an era of big changes for our family. I could try it out for a year. Ma had tired of her demanding career choices and was looking at options that might bring her back to Taipei. Her beautiful face, impacted by change and fatigue, shifted to a serious, concerned look when we discussed nonprofit, social justice work, and pay.

"Bei," she began, "real change begins in the belly of the beast."

I pondered what she said. Did she mean that I wouldn't make the most impact working at a nonprofit? I asked her as much, and she confirmed.

"Ma, are you saying I should consider working a corporate job?" I couldn't have felt further from the belly of the corporate beast at this point in my life.

She simply nodded, and then after a moment of reflection, added, "Have a mantel of excellence. And remember, don't let the bastards get you down."

I watched as she looked at her surroundings. It was a look of departure, of a vision that was building in her mind. As though she was manifesting her own move to come.

I made the difficult decision to take the leap and accept the job offer. I broke up with my girlfriend, who was a musician on tour. I hugged Sarah Pony and all my friends goodbye. I sold and parted with many of my belongings and packed up my beautiful brownstone apartment in Fort Greene. I parted ways with the flea market vendors I had befriended over the years. I went to my favorite restaurants and shared my news. I told my community this was the hardest thing I'd ever done. I hoped pursuing my career and investing in my future would be worth it.

Before I knew it, movers arrived and packed up the selected furniture and boxed items that would begin their long drive west. Alone in my empty brownstone, I was left with two suitcases and a few items to store at my parents' house. Ba borrowed his brother's van and picked me up. When he arrived, he saw my vulnerability and fear. I was in shock and terrified about what I was doing. Why had I made this decision? Why was I choosing to leave everyone—my home and community?

"Just one year," I told him with tears in my eyes.

Ba drove me to JFK International Airport. I thought about all the drives we had taken together. Drives to and from horse shows and the barn. Drives to and from IHOP during my teen years. That uncomfortable drive home after he followed me to that boy's house and I was pursued by that car of men. And now he was driving me to let me go and say goodbye. I suddenly longed for more car rides with Ba. It felt eerily final, him dropping me off while everything I owned was either sold, given away, or in transit.

Once my suitcases were at the curb, Ba gave me a hug, reminding me to keep my chin up. He was planning to fly out to help me in two weeks when the truck with my things would arrive at my doorstep. It took everything in me to turn around and wheel my bags to the check-in counter. My mind and body were at odds. My body said to run back to Ba and reverse this decision, get my apartment back, call the move off. My mind said to keep going. It felt surreal. As my body made one last attempt to abort the mission, my mind caught up to it. *What on earth am I doing?* There was no turning back now.

I LANDED in San Francisco seven hours later with puffy, swollen eyes from crying most of the overnight flight. I picked up my two suitcases from baggage claim and caught a cab to an apartment I had never seen but had put down a partial deposit for, thanks to a friend of a friend. The location was walking distance from the nonprofit I'd soon start working at and the monthly rent was a steal at $1,150 a month. It would be the first time I'd live alone in my own one-bedroom apartment. Despite those positives, when the cab pulled up to a sad-looking apartment complex, I called my brother. I needed support. He picked up immediately and listened to me panic.

"Jon, what the hell did your sister do?!"

He tried calming me down and reassuring me. He reminded me that he, Ma, and Ba were coming out to help me move in and adjust. The cab dropped me off in front of the apartment building and I looked up.

"Oh no. I think this could be a shithole." I was reminded of that room I rented in Portland and felt that same pang of worry. I wanted to go back to my apartment in Brooklyn. Back to my life!

Jon kept encouraging me. "Ing, don't overthink it. It's temporary. Just go upstairs and sign the lease."

The superintendent, a disheveled-looking fifty-something, led me into the building. The red carpets along the hallways and stairs had stains on them that looked like they had been there for decades. The entire hallway needed a paint job. Exposed lightbulbs made it seem like we were on the set of a creepy movie. Despite it being the morning, inside the apartment complex felt like perpetual evening. You couldn't tell what time of day it was.

The superintendent walked up to apartment 6. She opened the door. Tall ceilings and wood floors were a plus, but all I could see were blacked-out windows and evidence that it was likely a former crack den. The toilet was horrifying, and the state of the bathtub and kitchen weren't that far off. She opened one of the closets to show me a Murphy bed made of wrought iron and a sunken mattress.

I gasped. "Is that original?"

"Why, I think it is," she responded.

It would be one of the first items I'd have removed. But first, the whole place needed a deep cleaning. The super let me know the landlady would be outside to handle the paperwork and she gave me a moment alone. I called Jon back to tell him the state of the digs.

"Ing, just sign the lease, it will be okay," he kept saying.

I listened, took a breath, and went outside to find the landlady. She pulled up in a minivan and lowered the window, exhaling cigarette smoke telling me to "get in." From a stack of folders wedged on her dashboard, she drew a typed-up lease with carbon copies. I signed on the dotted line and handed her a check for the rest of the deposit and first month's rent. She told me she came to San Francisco with fifty dollars in her pocket. It was reaffirming. People came to San Francisco for opportunities, and that's what I was here for.

Back in the apartment, I cleaned and tried to map out where my furniture would go when it arrived later that month. I began looking up garage sales, and a colleague who'd referred me for my new role lent me her air mattress. I called my parents, crying. Ma caught a flight the next day.

I was relieved when she rang me saying she had landed. She took the BART train to Twenty-Fourth Street and when she arrived, I bear-hugged her and never wanted to let go. Ma winced. She had severe back pain I didn't know about.

"Ma, how did you travel that long flight with your back in this state?"

She gave me a smile and simply said, "Mommy's nice, nice baby."

I was worth it. I felt so loved and supported.

"Thank you, Ma. I really needed you here. Thank you."

I picked up her bag and, hand in hand, we walked the few blocks to my apartment. She struggled up the stairs with her back pain, and when she entered, she reviewed the state of the apartment.

"Ay-ya. Well, you have plenty of opportunity to make it your own and fix up the place." She looked down at the air mattress. "Bei, I can't sleep on that," she remarked, as she reached behind and rubbed her back.

Ma wasted no time calling up the Hilton downtown and booked us a room with two queens. We took the BART down to Powell Street and checked in. It was comfortable and just what we both needed. I slept feeling safe that Ma was there with me.

The next morning, we rented a car and drove around the city. We found a great garage sale in the Castro run by two gay men. Ma seemed to have fun chatting with the guys and helped me select items for my work-in-progress apartment. We found potted succulents at another garage sale. I found an art deco ceiling light on Craigslist and the seller was kind enough to agree to drop it off. His name was Dave, a Chinese man in his sixties who had grown up as an immigrant in Chinatown and had had success in the first tech boom. He owned a lighting store and loved restoring mid-century furniture, which happened to be my preferred aesthetic. He and his wife lived nearby in Eureka Valley. He looked at beautiful Ma and how she tenderly held my hand as we walked about. He offered to install the lamp the next day. He became my first friend in San Francisco.

As Ma's visit was wrapping up, she escorted me to my first day of work and met my new colleagues. She introduced herself proudly as my mother. One of my co-workers shared that she had seen us walking hand in hand and thought it was a sweet moment, to see the new director presented by her mother. I liked the feeling, now as an adult, of holding Ma's hand and her soothing support. It made me wonder: Would it have made a difference if Ma had walked me to the bus stop when I was a kid? Would she have shielded me from racist remarks? How would she have responded to witnessing someone call me "half piece of shit" or asking me, "What are you"?

How would Ma
have responded to
someone calling me
"half piece of shit"
or asking me,
"What are you"?

I wondered about that river of distance between us. In San Francisco, she was on my side of the riverbank, embracing me. She was being a caring mom in my time of need. Would she still be here, by my side, if she accepted *all* of me? It was a looming question I had yet to receive an answer to.

On the last night of Ma's visit, I took her out to eat at Mission Chinese Food. The food wasn't the traditional fare we expected, but we enjoyed it. The owner gave us freebies and remarked on how adorable we were as mother and daughter. It was a scene that perhaps she and I had always wanted.

As we wrapped up dinner before she headed to the airport for a red-eye, I held her hand and smiled at her until the pang of anticipated separation had me in tears.

"Be strong," she said.

"Ma Bao Bei, I love you," I responded in Mandarin.

"Ma Bao Bei. Love you so much it hurts," she replied, also in Chinese.

And off she went back to the East Coast—home.

EVERY DAY I went to work. And when I got home, I'd sit and watch the sun set and cry. Until, as promised, Ba arrived, with Jon to follow. I was so grateful. Another bear hug as I hoped to hold on to his presence, to family. Ba was instrumental in directing the movers as they brought in all my furniture and belongings into my apartment. He took me out to shop for groceries, hit up the hardware store while I was at work, and helped me install blinds and fix up the apartment.

The superintendent acknowledged the apartment needed major repairs but explained I'd have to eat some of the cost as they didn't have the budget to cover these improvements. And so, I paid to replace the terrible bathroom floor and got a new kitchen counter. I pushed for a replacement oven that could fit a roast and settled for a used one that would only close with a chair propped up against it. Ba installed dimmers and a second ceiling lamp. He even got zapped because of the out-of-date wiring in the building. I felt happy again in the presence of a family member and grateful for his support and acts of service.

When it was time for him to fly home, I bawled. I even chased after him a bit as he waved from the cab.

"Please, Ba, bring me with you!"

I saw his eyes glisten. "Ing, it will be okay, promise. I'll see you soon."

I watched the cab take him away through a sheet of tears smearing my view. How pure was I becoming after the fire I had walked through? Tears stained my face as I walked up the stairs to apartment 6. I flung myself on my bed that had once occupied my beautiful Brooklyn apartment. I could almost hear the springtime sounds from what was now somebody else's backyard. *Stay strong*, I heard Ma say. *It will be okay*, I heard Ba say. *This is temporary, Ing*, my brother said, all comforting me in my mind as I cried myself to sleep.

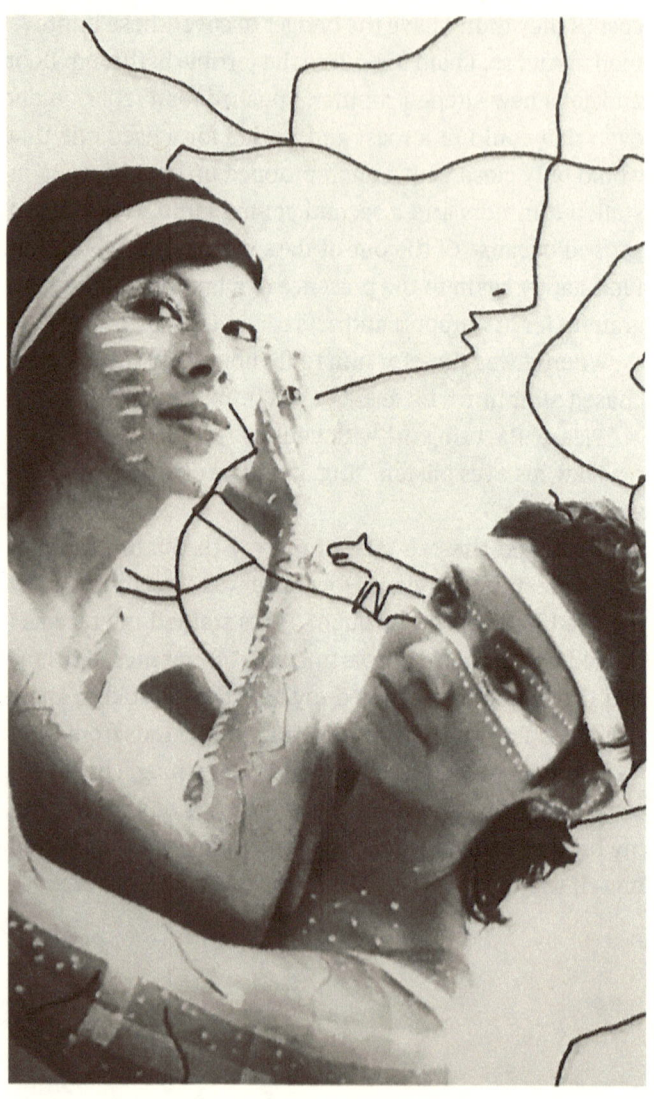

Photoshoot for Rad Pony's album cover with drawn designs by Shantell Martin.

top My first San Francisco Pride with Sarah Pony, 2011.
bottom Performing bass in Rad Pony in New York City. Photo by Bex Wade.

MORE THAN A WOMAN

Once the season of tears and longing for home passed, I regained my confidence and began to grow into this next chapter of my life. I made friends, found community, and established a network for my career. I joined an evening film course at the Queer Women of Color Media Arts Project (QWOCMAP) and made a film called *Faceplant* about moving to San Francisco as a hapa in search of her community. Part of the film includes random interviews in Dolores Park of people answering the question "What are you?" I wove in interviews with other mixed-race women and their stories about identity. It was invigorating and balanced the energy my busy day job required of me.

The woman who held the boom stand during film production was named Courtney. Over the past six months, she had become extremely important to me. But the universe had been trying to get us into each other's orbits for a lot longer.

She was a friend I had made through the queer scene over the years. I had known her long-term girlfriend from my touring days. Courtney and I had great conversations at girl parties and after-show engagements. One time, Boyskout bandmates and I even crashed a brunch she hosted. But we weren't in touch given we lived on different coasts. After I moved to San Francisco and the initial longing and lonely period passed, I started enjoying my bachelor pad and free ranging. And then, I ran into Courtney at a yoga class. When class was over, she came up to me and asked, "Ingrid? Ingrid Dahl? Do you live here now?"

I still had her same number logged in my contacts, and she had mine. I remembered her well-written music blog—she had such an understanding and feeling about music, even though she wasn't a practicing musician. At the time of that fateful yoga class, we were both still processing big changes we had each gone through in our lives. She had had a rough breakup with the girlfriend I had known. Running into her was a welcome reconnection.

The universe has a funny way of working. That June at Pride, Sarah Pony and Holly came to visit and join in the festivities. We kept running into Courtney, who also had friends visiting from Los Angeles who had gone to Yale with Sarah and Holly. It was the coincidental, truly organic setup rom-com movies are made of. I flirted openly at each party, but at the final event of the evening, something magical happened.

I was on the edge of the dance floor. Courtney came up to me just as the music suddenly shifted to a slow song. Holly and Sarah were dancing and looked over as they watched

Courtney bring over two drinks—one for me and one for her—and they smiled. It was the exact drink I had been ordering throughout the evening, complete with the two lemon wedges I liked. I watched the reflection of the disco ball dance on her face as I grinned, touched by her gesture.

Courtney was five feet nine and had a gender expression that was a mix of feminine and masculine, what we called a boy/girl. I suddenly noticed how handsome she was. Before I could thank her, she leaned down and kissed me. It was a special moment for all of us. For Courtney and me, it felt like we were wrapped in energy, a gravitational pull that had the effect of quieting all that surrounded us. My friends would later describe what a powerful, felt moment they'd witnessed: it was like seeing a time capsule unlock, like we had arrived at a pre-destined union. Being queer had never felt so good to me, and my heart pumped brighter, open and receiving, as I felt her lips against mine.

A week later, another special moment caught us by surprise at the Marin County Fair. Right before fireworks went off, I felt this unshakable truth. I was in love with her. I had never told anyone I was in love with them—I was saving that for the person I might marry. But I surprised myself with Courtney. Later that summer, she invited me as her plus-one to her good friend's wedding. It was a weekend affair and the morning after the nuptials, I told her how I was feeling and she said she felt it, too. She had qualities I didn't know I needed. She was encouraging, patient, and understanding. She was kind and everyone liked her for me. She had a solid career and an even greater integrity. She was creative and had a fire within her. She challenged

We saw one another, deeply, with the kind of admiration, respect, and aligned values that great love stories are made of.

me and waited for my trust issues to settle. She listened to me cry about how difficult workdays could be and she cheered me up with thoughtful gestures, often sending me flowers at my desk.

We had been together for six months when my eyes caught her smiling face as she held up the boom mic, and I knew my days of dating were over. I had fallen in love with her, and I could feel her love for me—in particular, how she *saw* me and all of me, and still loved every bit of who I was. We saw one another, deeply, with the kind of admiration, respect, and aligned values that great love stories are made of.

THAT FIRST CHRISTMAS after I moved to San Francisco, I brought Courtney to meet my family in New Jersey. Everyone loved her, even if Ma held her concerned expression firmly. She still believed this was a phase, and Courtney was challenging that notion for her. Ba was elated and gave me two thumbs-up. Jon was supportive, as was our extended family. Ma reminded me about my career and that I should focus on that. She didn't want me to get too serious.

"Ma, Courtney is my Gilbert Blythe," I countered, referencing her favorite films *Anne of Green Gables* and *Anne of Avonlea*. Her ears perked up, but the gravity of my truth was getting too real. She retreated to the other side of the riverbank.

Ba picked up on Ma's energy and started backing her, challenging me about Courtney's gender and how seriously I was taking the relationship. I challenged back, asking if he needed me to buy Courtney a soft pack to wear at the dinner table to make them more comfortable. My parents were aghast, as was I. I likened my situation to their own. They were an interracial couple that the world had seemed to be against; here I was, a woman in love with another woman, which was unconventional and outside social norms. Gay marriage hadn't been legalized, and yet interracial marriage was legalized thirteen years *after* my parents married. Their parents had been unsupportive of their union, just like they were now to me and my chosen partner. And just like my parents, Courtney and I felt marriage was where we were destined. We both had proposals in mind and felt excited about our life together.

After the holidays, Courtney moved in, and my parents announced that they were moving to Taipei. Before they moved, Courtney called my father, who was fond of traditions, to respectfully give him a heads-up that she planned to propose to me. He shared with her how he had no doubt that she was the person for me but warned her that my ma would take the news hard. We'd have a tough road ahead of us. I had no idea how tough it would be.

After a beautiful proposal and surprise weekend getaway, I called my parents to tell them the good news and Ba answered. It felt similar to that call where I tried coming out to Ma. He was quiet and distant, the opposite of celebratory.

"Ba, it's so exciting! Courtney proposed and I said *yes!*" I giddily shared.

He paused before unloading, coolly, "Your mother and I thought you'd make the *right* decision." Which, evidently, was to turn down Courtney's proposal. It was my turn to feel let down and disappointed. We ended the call, I cried into my fiancée's arms, and she held me through it. Both my parents were out of reach now.

Over the next few months, I tried to appeal to logic and reason. I reiterated how our experiences were in direct parallel. This time, it wasn't *white barbarian*, it was *yikes, a lesbian!* Even that reasoning couldn't unsettle their ironclad stubbornness against our decision to marry. A year passed and my parents and I didn't speak. My brother was concerned and frustrated with my parents, who, in his eyes, chose to create this division between us. My parents, now based in Taipei, had the geographical distance to add to the experience. Jon let me know that Ma was going through abrupt mood swings of extreme anger, dismissal, and despair. I would have told her she was not alone, but she chose to keep her distance.

One evening, Nai Nai Skyped me. Ma was in the background of the video call, and it was the first time I had seen her in more than a year. She didn't engage as Nai Nai spoke to me in broken English. She asked to meet Courtney. To my relief, she said she accepted us and supported our union. I looked over at Ma as happy tears streamed down my face. She was quiet, looking off camera. I wondered if she saw the similarities of this moment with her own experience—didn't she remember how it felt when her parents finally gave her their blessing to marry Ba?

That spring, we received news that Nai Nai's health was declining. I made plans to visit Taipei, and then more news came. Nai Nai had a stroke. Our fierce matriarch was left unable to communicate and confused. She cried, feeling lost, and was limited to a feeding tube. Soon, her heart gave out and, after several attempts to resuscitate her, she died.

In fall 2013, I flew out to attend her funeral. I walked the city thinking of Nai Nai and could hear her saying, *Study hard, be a good girl*, and the occasional, *Go to Washington, DC, and marry a senator*. She'd often call me "bao bei," or "little treasure," and tell me know how much she missed and loved me, how I was the firstborn of the Hu family's next generation. I missed her terribly. As I walked, I came across a store selling musical instruments and a guitar caught my eye. It reminded me of the time she had tried to set me up with the guitarist from her church. This comical episode started with her giving me an unexpected red envelope to buy a nice skirt for a party she was hosting that evening. I chuckled thinking of it now. How wrong that evening went for us both.

Nai Nai was in a tizzy by the time I returned with the skirt. "Hurry up, get ready!" I was about to show her what I found, but she just pushed me towards the hallway to change. "Make pretty!" Then she returned her attention to barking orders at the cook in the kitchen. The table had been set. *Wow, a party is going to happen*, I thought. Nai Nai rarely invited non-family members to her ornate apartment. Like Ma's, Nai Nai's space was a private sanctuary, used only on her terms, open irregularly outside of select family members. And so, a party was unusual.

I came out looking overtly feminine, a real departure from my more androgynous musician looks with my short hair and typical jeans and muscle tees. I didn't mind. I felt comfortable and playful. It was another costume, a performance, and I was used to that. Nai Nai and Ma clapped and overly admired how feminine I presented. Jon started to laugh, and Ba nudged him to quit it. I gave him a look.

"So, it's a party tonight..." I said, but before anyone could answer, the doorbell rang. Nai Nai rushed to get it, holding off her maid. She welcomed in a single dinner guest—a gentleman who had brought his guitar. He entered, paying his respects to Nai Nai and to the family seated at the table. Nai Nai introduced us: "*This* is my granddaughter." I stood there, shook his hand. There was no one else behind him. I looked at his guitar. I was confused. Where was the party?

Now Jon was really having a ball. He gave me a look that made me realize the reality of what was happening. *You are being set up, Ing.* I looked back at the scene in front of me. *Oh shit.*

"He plays guitar at our church. You play instruments, too. Also, guitar," Nai Nai quickly interjected.

If I wasn't so horrified, I would have softened and told Nai Nai how adorable she was in this moment of her eager, earnest hopefulness that this would magically be the meet-cute she could share in a speech at our future wedding. The guest and I exchanged glances. He seemed to pick up right away that not only was I not interested, but we also weren't each other's type. This would make for an interesting and strained dinner party. My brother had the most fun of everyone.

The guest never got to play guitar. I kind of just stared at him with a look that said, *Please end this awkward evening at your earliest convenience*. And to his credit, he took my message with the utmost respect. After dinner, he made up a reason that required his quick departure. Nai Nai allowed it, and after he left, she asked me what I thought.

"Thanks, Nai, but he's not my type," I responded, hugging her. She didn't leave much room for disappointment or being wrong, and so, she looked at me squarely in the eyes, pointing a finger up at me, and said, "Then, a SENATOR! Go to Washington!" She erupted in laughter, humming on her way back to the table with a toothpick in hand and the sound of success in her every step.

Nai Nai's funeral was epic on many levels. There was a lot of protocol and bowing required. They wheeled out my grandmother's embalmed body for us to pay our respects. I bawled as they wheeled her coffin to the front of the funeral event space with more floral arrangements than I had ever seen in my life. Hundreds of people came to pay their respects, including several adults who had grown up in Yi Kuang orphanage. I almost crumbled as they each cried out "Ma!" to my grandmother's corpse. And then my mother got up to the podium and gave a powerful speech. She was so strong through it all and delivered a message that moved people. I knew she felt like an orphan, and I could feel her crying out "Ma!"

After a day's worth of production and burial services, the four of us—my dad, mom, brother, and I—went on a short trip to get away from the city and the emotional toil plaguing us. But Ma was particularly distant. Several times she looked down at my engagement ring and looked away.

"Ma, do you like the ring Courtney got me? Isn't it beautiful?" My dear friend had made our rings, and this particular ring was a prototype.

Ma resisted, stubbornly. It's common to think your parent's reaction to an engagement would be happiness or tears of joy. My mom had no such reaction. Instead, she was spiteful. She gave me a wild look.

"Ma?" I asked, worried.

"I went to the top of my building and almost jumped off. Because you make such choices," she said, holding her gaze. My mind and heart short-circuited. Thoughts shot through my mind. Ma was suicidal? Then pain rippled through my circulatory system. She saw my choice to marry Courtney as a reason to commit such a devastating act.

Before I could respond, she kept going. "I have stage-one endometrial cancer and just had a surgery to remove everything. Plus, radiation."

Before I could let out a cry at her news and show how shocked I was to have missed this during our difficult phase of not speaking, she raised a finger at me.

"You *choosing* this life, you *being* gay, *gave* me cancer."

To say I was gutted is an understatement. Thankfully, my instinct was to reject her words and not let them pierce me any further.

"I will not accept that blame, Ma. I am *not* the cause of your cancer. I reject this."

The echo of her words kept knocking at my consciousness. She blamed my truth for her dissatisfaction with her life and for her cancer.

During the long flight home, I realized that getting married to Courtney was my decision and mine alone. I didn't choose my sexuality, but I absolutely chose Courtney as my person. I loved her, was in love with her, and she was my chosen family. I also loved my mom, but she was in no state to see clearly. I already knew that Ma, and likely Ba, would not be attending the wedding. And a year later, I was proved right. They did not come.

A YEAR AFTER Courtney and I were married, we bought our first home in San Francisco. Courtney was working at a global tech company, and I had moved into a leadership role in public media. Thanks to our network of female friends and sponsors, I had an opportunity to transition to a design education team at my first corporate for-profit company. We supported each other as we were challenged and took big leaps in our careers.

Jon kept my parents informed of our success and how, in marriage, Courtney's and my relationship deepened. We had become best friends, wives, and one another's family. Although we had support from our siblings, aunts, and uncles, we had let go of wanting my parents' approval and moved on. Ba periodically reached out to wish us well; he missed us and struggled oscillating between Ma and his daughter. Ma seemed to feel the shift in our energy and start to consider that if she didn't make an active effort, she might lose her daughter, forever. Somehow, she came to the realization that holding steadfastly to her position, her disappointment, and deep pain was not worth that loss. She wanted to be in our lives.

Of course, we didn't know at the time that this shift was happening with Ma, and that she and Ba were having deep conversations about re-engaging with us. I hadn't spoken to Ma. Not before the wedding and not after. And so, I was surprised to receive a phone call from her soon after we moved into our new house in 2015, a year after our wedding. Ma asked if she and Ba could spend the upcoming holiday with us, three months from now, in celebration of our new home. She seemed uncertain about how we would react but clear that a yes was what she hoped for. She asked again, "Could Mommy and Daddy come visit you?" I caught Courtney's glance and could tell that she was supportive.

"Ma, of course you and Ba are always welcome," I responded calmly, with a sigh of relief in my belly and heart. *Ma and Ba would spend Christmas with us, me and my wife, in our home.* Was I dreaming? I missed them and felt a rise of longing to be held by my parents, anticipating their arrival. We set dates and they booked flights. Jon, our forever supporter, would be joining, too. He was devotedly by my side throughout our family fracturing—he actively defended me and tried to reason with my parents, and on our big day, he held our rings and gave, hands down, one of the best speeches I've ever heard. I could tell now that he, too, felt relief in my parents' decision to fly back from Taipei to spend the holidays with us. It was hope of reconciliation within our grasp.

We awaited my parents' visit with anticipation and uncertainty. Courtney and I were open, albeit a bit cautious, but when they arrived, we hugged them for the first time as wives. It felt like a new embrace. We ate, connected, sat by our fireplace, and I watched as the light from the embers danced across Courtney's and Ma's smiling faces. The warmth of the fire paled in comparison to the love pouring within and around me. Ma and Ba had joined my new family.

The morning of Christmas Eve, Ma gave an unexpected toast. She stood holding her glass, looking at us with sincerity.

"I am so sorry Mommy and Daddy didn't come to your wedding. We were shortsighted and we love you. We want to be part of your lives..." She paused and I could see tears welling up in her eyes, which snapped me out of my chair. I ran to her and wrapped her in my embrace.

She closed the gap between us. She chose me; I was no longer rejected nor abandoned. There would be no more threats or manipulation through disappointment. Our souls seemed to meet in the flesh for the first time without holding back. Love drawing us together, I held her head gently against my neck and reached down to hold her hand.

"I forgive you, I love you," I said. "No matter what. You are my ma." I could almost hear her soul reply, as if I were a child: *Mommy's nice, nice baby.*

Ba came up and hugged Courtney and Jon before they took Ma and I in an embrace.

"Ma Bao Bei. We love you," she expressed. We shed tears of reunion and love. I finally had my family back and they were joining my chosen family. I was relieved, dancing across disbelief and joy. A new era was born in that moment. One where my truth was honored and accepted.

After a week together, before their visit ended, I caught a scene that will forever stay in my heart: Ma holding hands with Courtney, walking down the street. It was a moment my heart doubled, a feeling I will never forget. Her expression of tender affection showed me that she loved me, all of me, so very much—and extended that tenderness and

A new era was
born in that moment.
One where my
truth was honored
and accepted.

care to the person whom I loved, regardless of their gender. We moved forward, together, as a family from that day on.

OVER THE NEXT few years, Courtney and I made multiple trips to Taipei to visit family. We connected weekly with them back in California and caught up on life events. As Ma had at one point done, I, too, climbed the career ladder. I transitioned to roles in big tech, thanks again to female sponsors in my network and friend group. I did what Ma guided me to do. I went into the belly of the beast and tried to make change. Naively, I thought that my experience would be better than hers either because we were in corporate settings decades apart and social inequities must have changed or because I was half white. Yet, in key instances, we were both swallowed whole and spat out like garbage. Making change in the belly of the beast was not easy and, at times, impossible.

And then we arose from the ashes. After I was spat out, I realized I had let work become too tied to my identity. I eventually rebuilt myself; I got a certificate in leadership coaching and started my own consulting business working with clients, which led to full-time roles overseeing leadership development at large companies.

Ma left her corporate role in Taipei that made her miserable. After having a hysterectomy and radiation therapy, she decided to work at Yi Kuang orphanage, which led her to pursue her third master's degree in social work. Ma's treatment burned and scarred her; she didn't like feeling physically week and having to slowly regain her strength. And so she decided to go to the gym three days a week. Over time, she became the most physically fit I had ever seen her. She was independent, traveling across the city via subway, meeting up with Ba for dinner, and waking up to enjoy breakfast before heading out to class, work, and the gym. She loved being a student again. Her doctors consistently said her cancer was almost in remission. That scary moment of stage-one endometrial cancer appeared to be in the rearview mirror. All felt right.

COURTNEY AND I had just parked outside a restaurant in wine country one date night when my cell phone rang. I stared at Ba's name on the display, wondering what kind of news he had to share. I was about to let the call go to voicemail when I glanced back up at Courtney. Her warm hazel eyes encouraged me to pick up the call and not worry if it made us late to our reservation.

"Wei? Ba?" I answered, placing the call on speaker. It was early in the morning in Taipei.

"Ing . . . " There was an eerie pause.

"Ba?" I wasn't sure if the connection was spotty.

He let out a desperate sigh with the words traveling after him: "The cancer is back."

"What? What do you mean?" I asked. There was a second pause. A bolt of emotion shot into my eyes and tears welled. I needed to know information. What kind of cancer? Was it the same? How much was back? What did this mean for Ma, for us? As these thoughts came fast and furiously, I heard her cough. That cough stopped my thoughts dead in their tracks.

"Bei, I have stage four. Now in my lungs," Ma stammered. I could hear her muffled tears; she was holding them in.

Then I was bawling. Courtney started to tear up as she held my hand. She looked at me as if she was preparing a security blanket to catch me as the news continued to unfold.

"The oncologist is performing many tests, bei. I know, this is disappointing..." She trailed off, unable to finish the sentence. My heart sank farther than it ever had before. Ba chimed in. "Ing, let's connect tomorrow when we have more information." But at that point, I already knew that tomorrow's news would be a headline newsworthy for all time. We ended the call, and it started to rain.

With all the tears flowing inside the car, it was fitting that the clouds followed. It was as if my insides were exposed, there for nature to amplify. I held on to that moment because I could hear the rush of pain, fear, anticipatory grief, panic, and desperation galloping towards center stage. It was the quiet before the storm. Just listening to nature cry with me, surround and engulf me, gave me a sense of connection in a moment when I was so physically distant from Ma and Ba.

My special date night with Courtney in wine country took a turn after that. We made the best of dinner at a restaurant that had a beautiful, glass-encased courtyard and a dreamy, whimsical feeling. It was the kind of restaurant I would want to take Ma to when she visited next. *Would that happen?* I wondered. I found myself getting lost in trying to guess how much time we had left with her. The weight of the news made my worst-case-scenario anxieties cave in on me. I'd always be wondering how much time she had left.

Courtney held my hand as she drove us back home to San Francisco. Her father died tragically in a motorcycle accident when she was in her early twenties, just a few years before we met while I was on tour. It was tragic and traumatizing, and over the years I witnessed the eruption of uncontrollable pain and yearning for her dad. Once, at a Chinese restaurant, she exploded into a sea of tears. Certain moments surprised and confused her with a tsunami of sensations. These outbursts of longing to have her dad back were so real. She wanted to have him here with us in the physical world, which he was extracted from too soon.

I reflected on what Courtney must have gone through in her parallel, yet radically different experience. One moment her dad was alive and thriving in his mid-forties, living up his life as a single father of three children who were all entering adulthood. The next, he was gone. Forever. There was no chance to say goodbye, no processing how long he had left, whether he *might* leave or stick around, which was the cruelty I faced with cancer moving into my mom's lungs. Learning Ma's cancer was back suffocated hope and filled the air with the *possibility* of losing her. I was processing the vast unknown, the anticipation, the waiting—and welcoming, with it, the fear and desperation that comes from life-threatening illness.

It was the power of the news that shook my insides like an earthquake. As if dark matter and gravity collided in a way you could see and feel, yet the limitations of my human eyes could make out only a blur at most through all the tears and rain on the windshield as we drove back to the city.

Ba must have sensed that I needed more information and so he began texting me and Jon. There were more tests and treatments to figure out with the oncologist, and they would keep us informed. All they really knew was one, heavy fact: this mutation was *aggressive*. The tumors in her lungs were like cracks in concrete. In Taiwanese culture, people are superstitious about writing a will because they believe it's like *willing* your death to happen. Because of that, we were slow to realize that no doctor would share an actual prognosis. In some ways, a piece of me is still stuck in that moment in the car in the rain, hand in hand with my wife, listening to the news—frozen in the unraveling of a horrible truth.

WITH CANCER, it can feel like every step you take requires crossing a channel between two cities. Travel that was once direct and streamlined becomes complicated and puts you in a state of terror. Each step seems to take you farther away from your destination, even though you could have sworn you just saw the shore. With cancer, a multitude of barriers get in your path. Going from point A to B now includes a series of obstacles. Each data set, each CT scan result has you one moment riding a pendulum; the next, in solitary confinement. It's as if you are living in a waking nightmare. You're on a rollercoaster while also in a waiting room. And you're very much awake, in an anxious state.

You start forgetting that there was ever a channel to cross between two cities. You're so focused on making sense of where you are in this squiggly line of a surrealist painting that makes no sense unless you're the artist. Cancer is the artist holding the brush, the mad scientist at the helm, an unannounced roommate whom you can't confront, communicate, reason with, or inform that they have overstayed and were never welcomed. Cancer trespasses, harms, robs. It was a sociopath that Ma was forced to live with, that was encased in her body, and we stood outside trying to protect her without a blueprint to follow or a way to break Ma out.

The irony is, had we broken in, we would have found Ma sitting on a sofa watching HGTV. Somehow, Ma made the decision *not* to be caught up in the ramifications of her cancer. She chose to ignore it entirely and not know the medical details. She would live on her terms. She took on a mind-set that she would make a full recovery—her faith and belief were strong and beautifully naïve. She met the sociopath with her own degree of disassociation. *Of course, I'll recover*, she'd say. She would heal and this would be a thing of the past. In fact, her faith in God would heal her. She was sure that God, the Sky Daddy, would take a moment away from His busy schedule and notice that His loyal and devoted servant was in need. He would attend to her, surely.

In the meantime, Ma agreed to take an aggressive course of chemo. She also ramped up her coursework in her master's program at the top university in Taipei. She immersed herself in reading, studying, and writing papers. Ba would review the English versions for grammatical errors and corrections, while balancing consulting work and his devout research on clinical trials and immunotherapy options for Ma.

When she started losing her hair, she had it shaved off and bought a quality wig with real hair. She disregarded her

You're so focused on making sense of where you are in this surrealist painting that makes no sense unless you're the artist.

sociopath, disguised its effects, and flirted with ignorance. She fought its terror with her thirst for knowledge. She was motivated to finish her degree and did not tell anyone outside her family about the sociopath in her life.

As a family, we rallied, managed, and tempered our fears. We waltzed with Ma's dream-like vision of the future and thought about how we'd be all together again back in the United States when she fully recovered. She began expressing her desire for grandchildren and we had to have a few hard conversations.

"Ma, Courtney and I have made the decision to be child-free. We don't want to have kids."

She'd try to persuade, resist, or ignore. Then she'd reach into her pocket and find that old friend, guilt trip, and toss it to me.

"Do you want me to die without ever meeting my grandchild?"

A guilt bomb. It took time for me to respond and push aside the pressure to please her with honesty and integrity.

"Ma, if I ignored Courtney's and my decision, bulldozing our lives to bring a child into the world just to make you happy, what would happen if you die? We would be left with a child we did not want and a tarnished relationship. Is that what you want?"

Silence.

I knew what she was thinking. As much as that sounded like something she *wouldn't* want me to experience, she'd still prefer the kid. Before shifting her grandkid desires to my brother, she surprised me. She told me how science had made great advances and there were plenty of ways

Courtney and I could start a family together as a lesbian couple. My mouth was agape.

"Wow, Ma. How far you've come!"

That wasn't her only surprise. Her second was an announcement that she had accepted a summer internship in San Francisco, and she would be spending the upcoming summer with us. She was thrilled and assumed we would match her excitement. We had little advance warning that she was planning an internship in a few weeks, let alone back in the States away from her doctors, treatments, and, most important of all, Ba.

I wondered why she hadn't brought this up until now, if she just assumed we'd adjust our lives to prioritize her scholastic activities. We were in the middle of negotiating a home remodel project that would have workers accessing the backyard through the lower part of the house. Would the house be ready? How would Courtney take the news? She wasn't used to family visitors for more than a few days or a long weekend. Several things had to be organized and planned out, I explained.

"No problem, Bei! I'll see you in a few weeks," Ma said, shrugging. Click. She had hung up.

I waited for Courtney to get back from her busy job to let her know about Ma's plans. I took a deep breath. It was an imposition, but it was my mom, who was battling cancer. How could she refuse?

After a lot of conversations with Courtney, Ba, and my brother, we planned and prepared for Ma's arrival.

A few weeks later, she began her first day as our housemate. She was full of energy, excited for her internship—and eager to be spending time with us when none of us were working. As we showed her the new guest suite that had been completed in time for her arrival, I asked her, "What time does your internship start?"

"Tomorrow at 5 a.m."

"What?! 5 a.m.? Tomorrow?"

"I am answering the suicide hotline, ten minutes with each caller, and no one wants to take that shift. So, interns fill that gap."

I tried picturing Ma answering calls from elders who were considering suicide. But she was the forever-holder of the talking stick. Would she talk through their entire call?

That was the least of my worries. The next morning, Ma walked up from the lower den where she slept and into the kitchen. There, she boiled water, clanged dishes, and opened and closed the fridge multiple times. She then walked down the stairs, sliding her hand along the banister, before fumbling around, collecting her bag, putting on her shoes, and opening and closing the garage door. Courtney and I lay awake, having heard every single movement. She turned to look at me. "All summer?" she asked. All I could do was nod and say I'd see if she could negotiate a later shift.

Ma returned in the afternoon and helped herself to whatever was in the kitchen, then sat down and watched HGTV with her laptop and notes spread out on the coffee table. I came home and, seeing she was busy, checked the fridge to prep for dinner. What was once full was now empty. I took a deep breath. I was tired. The house felt out of harmony with the introduction of Ma and her spreading out all over it, consuming a week's worth of food in a day.

"Hey, Ma, what happened to all the food?"

She mentioned she may have eaten, well, all the yogurt and fruit, the items for lunch, and possibly a bit more. Then she paused before asking, "Are you going to make dinner? I'm hungry." I couldn't believe it. Such a mix of reactions rose within me—I felt like laughing, but I also felt frustrated, mixed with feeling amazed and impressed with her appetite. She was like a teenager.

Ma had become the kid we said we never wanted. Although I was still very much her daughter, I felt like I was playing the parent role. We, my wife and I, had become her gay parents. That got me chuckling out loud. She looked at me pensively, then wiggled her foot and did a little seated dance. She knew the moment of possible upset had passed.

"When Courtney gets home, let's go out to dinner." She gave me two thumbs-up and hummed a tune contentedly as I placed a big order for groceries to refill our nearly empty fridge.

IN THE WEEKS that followed, Ma came home with great stories from her internship. She spoke with elder trans and queer persons, and elders who were lonely and sad and considering ending their lives. Within ten minutes of connecting with my mom, they said they felt soothed and uplifted. In the best cases, they left the call with a new sense of hope and perspective. She even brought the love of Jesus to one old Asian woman whom she spoke with weekly. Over the course of that relationship, the nai nai—as Ma called her—found community in place of the family that had somehow forgotten about her.

Ma's most insightful conversation was with a Jewish man who immediately called out her Taiwanese accent. She pushed through that initial wave of trauma memory—all those years of re-recording her voicemails to smooth out the ridges of her accent, the giveaway that she didn't fully belong as a woman in power—and let it go so that she could connect with this caller. In the end he, too, felt her grace and connection, and thanked her for helping him. When Ma shared this with me, I was amazed by her growth and my eyes swelled up in tears. I hugged her.

"I'm so proud of you, Ma." And I meant it with every fiber of my being. Ma, tormented by this American life, was transformed. She was the purest of gold.

One day Ma came to visit me at work, and my team and co-workers brought her gifts and flowers. They had been with me on my mom's cancer journey, giving me support and space to cry. They treated me as if I were still me, even though I hadn't felt like myself since the cancer news broke.

Ma wore a special outfit and her pretty wig given that the chemo treatments had taken her hair; she was all smiles and delighted everyone, as if we were right back in Paris with my study-abroad peers. She gave compliments, hugged everyone, and enjoyed the free cappuccinos and snacks on every floor. Ma knew I was working on big cultural shifts at work and co-creating workshops to increase self-awareness and curiosity so that people could grow, connect, and relate across difference.

She was proud to learn about my work and was especially interested in my own learning moments. One such moment was when another senior leader, an older white male peer of mine, said, "Ingrid, you're *so* exotic." I thought about the person I had become. Much like Ma's transformative reaction to the caller who pointed out her accent in a rude, even accusatory manner, I met my peer with grace and curiosity. First, I let him know that word was triggering for me. He was shocked: "Triggering?" I told him how I'd spent decades of my life listening to people use that word to describe me, what it meant, and the pain it inflicted on me. I gently explained the connotations that came with that word when white people use it to express desire or fascination with otherness. He said that he truly meant to compliment me. I understood, thanked him, and shared alternative options that are meaningful to me. When Ma heard about this conversation, she was elated that this co-worker and I had connected in this way. It deepened our friendship and mutual respect.

During Ma's stay, I wasn't always on my best behavior, nor was I always my most transformed self. There were times I was frustrated and emotional—moments I felt caught between Courtney and Ma, who would each ask me to communicate with the other on their behalf. There were a lot of demands on my time. Did I spend enough time with Ma but not enough time with Courtney? It was a bizarre balancing act. I was caught between two women I loved and their expectations and needs—whether real or perceived.

Once, I even overheard Ma talking to Ba on the phone about how good I had it. That when she hosted Nai Nai, she'd have to meet her mother's every need—as per their agreement when she'd visit the States. I confronted Ma about what I overheard, and her face twisted. She'd been caught in the act of talking shit.

"Ma, I don't think that's fair to say and it's upsetting. Yes, our relationship is different from yours and Nai Nai's. But I hope you see that I *am* dutiful and support you, even if that's not in the same way you had to respond to Nai Nai's demands that you serve her and listen to her every request."

Ma wanted me to give her the same respect Nai Nai craved from her. I encouraged her to consider how we all wanted the same thing and that maybe we already had it.

One afternoon when I wasn't at my best, I got fed up with having another full sink of dishes to wash. I had been picking up the extra glasses and mugs that Ma would leave throughout the house, and I was annoyed that I had become her resident dishwasher. There were pans filling the sink. I was reminded of that one roommate back in college who never cleaned any of her dishes.

"Ma, you need to clean your dishes!" I said, lashing out.

I felt heat rising to my cheeks. I was flush with irritation. She hopped to her feet, came over, and apologized. But then, yet again, she surprised me. She looked down, as if in shame. I paused, watching her face change. I could feel my face cooling down.

"I, I can't pick up the pans," she almost whispered. It took me a moment to understand what she was saying: she felt so physically weak that she couldn't pick up a frying pan to wash it. She had never let on the effect chemo had on her body. That meant the sink made her confront the harsh reality of what her body was going through with cancer. *She couldn't even pick up a pan* and I had no idea. I hugged her and wept briefly, but the tears continued forever internally. Ma, the strongest person I knew, couldn't even lift a pan. *Fuck the dishes, Ma. I love you.*

AS MA'S INTERNSHIP came to an end, I made plans to take several days off work to spend with her. I went to her final internship day. The nonprofit director and team had organized a little party, and Ma delivered a presentation that reflected her summer experiences answering the suicide hotline. Ma was studying how robotics designed to support the elderly could provide comfort and physical warmth and help with loneliness, particularly towards the end of life.

During her presentation, she was animated but coughed a lot, and, as usual, tried to pass her cough off as a slight cold. Ma and the director had bumpy moments, but ultimately, Ma respected her. The director didn't know Ma had stage-four cancer, and so she was tougher on her than she would have been had she known.

Ma gave the director a thank-you card and asked me to deliver it to her as she was packing up. I knocked on the director's office door, which was ajar. She waved me in, looking surprised. I handed her the card and thanked her for affording Ma the opportunity to intern with the team. I looked at her, this busy and competent woman, and my eyes began to water.

"You probably don't know this, but I'm especially thankful because my mother has stage-four cancer. And, well, this may be the last time you ever see her again."

I started to walk back towards the door but turned to see her reach for a box of tissues. Even she loved my mother.

The last few days with Ma were so special. She and I went to what had become her favorite boutique thrift store, where she picked up several items to pack for her return trip to Taipei. We walked through flower gardens throughout San Francisco and the South Bay. I took her to Foster City to have lunch with her friends, none of whom knew about her condition. I made dinner, we watched movies, and while we were out and about, we often held hands. The same hands that guided me to the first day of my big job in San Francisco. The same hands that held me up when the challenge of moving to a new city felt overwhelmingly difficult and lonely. The same hands that accepted and loved my wife.

Here she was, finishing up her graduate studies with an internship, and I got to hold her hand through it all. It felt tender to have her present, to hug her, to meet her smile with love, consideration, and care. The roaring river between two riverbanks was a thing of the distant past. We connected, felt seen and considered, appreciated and understood. The pictures I took of her during those few precious days were magical. I often wish she and I spent the entire summer together, neither of us working, just spending each day like those few final ones—when she was so vibrant and alive, despite her intensifying cough that pushed my anxiety to new heights.

On our final day together as a housemate unit of three, Ma gave us a card. Courtney had gifted her an LGBTQ shirt from her company, and Ma put it on immediately. We had taken her to get tacos for lunch, which she ate like dumplings. She was adorable and full of smiles and laugher.

"Hey, Ma, where would you like to get dinner later tonight?" I asked. "It will be your last dinner in San Francisco."

"A HAMBURGER!" she replied, giddily with a big, beaming grin. We took her to Hamburger Mary's in the Castro neighborhood and a drag queen served her a grand cheeseburger and fries. I took a photo of her taking a bite of that large burger. She was all smiles with the setting sun sparkling in the corners of her eyes, wearing her LGBTQ T-shirt, and lightly flirting with a gay man. She had come so far, my Ma. The purest gold, exceeding herself.

Courtney and I get married in September 2014.

top Ma and her housemates.

bottom Ma's last dinner in San Francisco.

All united as a family in San Francisco. Photo by Jon Dahl.

九

QUARANTINE DIARIES

WHEN I HUGGED MA goodbye at the airport, I felt a tug as she coughed from my embrace. It was as if my future self was giving me a heads-up that this would be the last time I'd ever hold this healthy version of her. Ma got on the plane, and fifteen hours later, she made it safely back to Taipei and reunited with Ba. I sat in our home, feeling like an empty nester, yet basked in the return of harmony in our space originally meant for two. I knew Ma would acclimate to her routines and continue working on her final thesis for her master's degree. We all hoped that Ma's drive to complete her degree would keep the sociopath at bay. Then right before the winter holidays, I got another phone call.

Ma had had a routine CT scan, and it came back with bad news. Unbeknownst to her, the sociopath had made progress, taking over more space in her body. Ma had pleural effusion, which meant the cancer-cell fluid was filling the space between her lungs and her chest wall. Ba had done research on pleural effusion, but he couldn't bring himself to talk about how much time patients had left to live once diagnosed. I had to look it up and it was dumbfounding: eight to twelve months.

Ma's cough persisted. Her largest tumor—what we all ended up calling the "death star"—was misbehaving, rebelling. It was inching closer to her bronchial pathway, dangerously close to her throat. Courtney and I booked a flight to go see her in March. At the same time, the world was catching its own illness, as if poetically sympathizing with Ma. I had just celebrated my fortieth birthday, and a global pandemic caused by COVID-19 had taken the world stage. What was terrifying about this pandemic was that it disproportionately affected people like my mother—those suffering from cancer, struggling to breathe, and requiring access to oxygen. Ma stayed at home. She continued to write her thesis and accepted the assistance of a full-time oxygen machine.

COVID was like a mythical dragon, flying around the world, dosing us with great variations of illness. Some people died without getting the chance to say goodbye to their family, as their loved ones waited outside the hospital. Entire countries shut their borders, including Taiwan, making it impossible for my brother, Courtney, and me to enter. The trip in March 2020 would never happen.

We did significant research to try to find a pathway into the country. We waited to apply for special entry visas for people with relatives living in Taiwan. When applications finally opened, Jon and I submitted our requests *immediately* to the Taipei Economic and Cultural Office (TECO), sent money and our passports, and hoped that we'd be accepted. A month went by. At long last, Jon and I received our passports with the visa included. We had about twenty-four hours to get a PCR test to prove we were negative for COVID-19, book a flight, and secure a quarantine hotel.

In advance of receiving our special entry visas, we researched more than 120 hotels in Taipei that were under the government's new "quarantine hotel" provision. In our research, we found a Google spreadsheet that included all the approved quarantine hotels with links to identify location, price point, availability, and room options. Once we landed, we would be required to head to our reserved quarantine hotel and stay there for fifteen days. No human contact, a prisoner in your room. Three meals per day would be delivered outside your room. The police would call daily to check that your temperature was normal and your provided COVID at-home test-kit results were negative.

I braced myself and thought about how I could mentally survive two weeks with no human interaction, no ability to leave the hotel room, and my desperation to get to Ma. I'd have to overprepare, go dry-goods shopping, pack things to help if the room smelled, and seek out a room that had a window that could be opened or, better yet, a balcony to breathe in fresh air and feel the sun on my face. I'd have to save money, sign up for family medical leave, negotiate with my boss, and set my team up for success while I was gone. There was an endless amount of preparation to be done.

Meanwhile, Ma was almost done with her thesis and graduation was in sight. We were all so grateful. It was her dream to finish this degree, and now it was in reach. She was the top student of her entire class, and the only one secretly battling an aggressive cancer.

When we told Ma we were on our way to her, she requested we not come. That stung at first, an old pang of rejection feeling like a new wound on the surface of my skin. She explained: It was too cumbersome and dangerous. She didn't want us to bring COVID to her or Ba. Jon and I agreed. But we had an opening, a window of opportunity to see her, and we were going no matter what.

Jon got to his quarantine hotel first. He sent me a text about how disorienting and chaotic his experience was upon arrival at the airport. Once their plane landed, he and the rest of the passengers needed to show a negative PCR test and provide a phone number for the police to track their location and check in on their health status. Jon didn't speak Mandarin. That additional barrier got us all worried. But he managed to get through the many unforeseen steps, got ushered into a quarantine taxi, and made it to his hotel. He was grateful that he arrived at night, especially once he was told that the countdown of fifteen days would begin the day after arrival. None of the rules made sense, but given how new they were and how unknown everything else felt, people clung to protocol.

The night before my flight, Courtney watched me go through my mega-packed suitcase. We made a lasagna—Ma's favorite—to eat as my last meal before I left. Since she wasn't related to Ma by blood, Courtney wasn't eligible to go to Taiwan. Only I could get the special entry visa. She dropped me off at the airport, encouraging me, calming me as I felt anxious. I looked at her, admiring how strong she was, and suddenly felt overwhelmed by the journey ahead. I wrapped my arms around her and hugged her tightly, taking a deep whiff of her scent. I didn't want to be separated from her. I already missed her, and our home, terribly. It felt like a major departure. I was reminded of the same feeling I had at the curb of the airport before I moved to San Francisco. I couldn't stay. I had to get to Ma.

The next day, I landed in Taipei bracing myself for chaos in the airport. It was just as Jon had described. Trying to navigate the airport with all these checkpoints, paperwork, and tracking procedures was so confusing. My limited Chinese didn't help much. I huddled close to the other passengers who spoke only English. We saw that passengers who tested positive for COVID were immediately taken to quarantine medical facilities. I'd heard that when that happened, you could get held for about a month—where exactly, no one seemed to know. I wanted to avoid that as much as possible. Not just because of how scary that was, but because I had a single objective: get to Ma.

I barely had a moment to breathe in the familiar scents of Taiwan when I exited the airport, as I was quickly ushered to the queue of quarantine taxis. I handed the details for my approved quarantine hotel to an officer. Shortly after that, my luggage and I were sprayed head to toe with some kind of chemical. A driver in a hazmat suit walked around the taxi to open the door. The entire inside was lined with plastic and there was a divider between driver and passenger. As I sat watching the rain begin to fall, smearing my view, I wished I could open the window. The journey was but a watercolor of lights and silhouettes.

Having called ahead to indicate my arrival, I was dropped off at the basement level of the hotel. I was sprayed again head to toe by a hotel representative, who was also wearing a hazmat suit. They escorted me into the elevator, their gloved hands selecting my floor number, the buttons covered with plastic, and then handed me a small piece of paper with my room number. I was instructed that the door to my room would be ajar, and I was to enter and immediately shut and lock the door behind me.

After following the instructions, I was relieved to see the room included what I'd reserved and paid extra for: a separate living room and a balcony. The phone and light switches were all covered in plastic. On the coffee table was a brand-new thermometer, which I was instructed to use to verify my temperature when the hotel and police called me daily. I looked at both rooms and started mentally charting out spaces for various things: bedroom for sleeping, living room corner for working out, couch and coffee table for eating, desk for working and watercoloring—the art supplies a gift from a friend of mine. Thankfully, Ba had dropped off a care package earlier in the day for my arrival, and I had fresh produce to add to the dry goods I brought with me.

I looked back at the door locked from the inside and felt like a high-profile prisoner. That door would keep me from any human interaction for the next two weeks. I would never see the person who dropped off my government-sponsored daily meals outside my door; nor whoever picked up the trash I was instructed to tie up and leave outside my door in the evenings.

I had to tell myself, the girl who always loved leaving Nai Nai's apartment every day to explore the city, that no,

The journey
was but a
watercolor of lights
and silhouettes.

I could not leave. I had to make this work. On the wall, I tacked up a piece of paper from my notebook. Tomorrow would be day one, which I'd mark with a single vertical line. Eventually, I'd see three sets of five marks, but for now, it would remain blank. I stacked my books, watercolors, yoga mat, and the small weights I had brought with me; I set up the microkitchen with provisions; I set up all my toiletries in the bathroom, hung a preemptive makeshift laundry line, and unpacked. Finally, I opened the door from the bathroom that led to the dangerous-seeming balcony and looked down at the ground, far below. I wondered, *Has anyone in quarantine ever jumped?* And, of course, I thought of Ma.

THOSE FIFTEEN DAYS in quarantine were surreal. At one point, I started choking on a long piece of cooked onion and realized that no one would come to help me. I had to reach down my throat, locate the thread of onion, and pull it out to survive. And that wasn't the only occasion that piqued my sense of survival and fear.

One morning, what sounded like a fire alarm went off. I wasn't sure whether I could leave the room, given that earlier that week another quarantine guest had left their room and triggered the alarm. We were told that should we leave our rooms, we risked being sent back to the airport to immediately depart the country. I still don't know what happened to that guest, but I longed for the freedom, however brief, they might have had. After looking through the peephole and not seeing a soul, I slid down from the door onto the floor and held my knees as the alarm kept on threatening and warning. I walked to the balcony and my fear of heights tickled my arms and thighs. I stared down at the cars, the people, the life happening below. *Just a few more days*, I told myself. I walked back into the room where the shabby piece of paper hung as my calendar, ready for me to scratch off another day. The time difference didn't help. My friends, family, and wife back in the US were not yet awake. Ba was busy taking care of Ma, who was low on energy and getting significantly weaker. She relied completely on that oxygen machine. I needed to keep it together. I was so close to the finish line.

Jon, who spent his days sleeping after working east-coast hours, got released first. I was relieved when he and Ba came to my hotel to wave at me from street level. I was higher up than I would have liked. I pressed myself against the window, trying to contort my head to look down at their little figures below. A pang of desperation at wanting to be with them rose through me. We talked on the phone, and I cried. "Please get me out of here," I begged. They reasoned with me, sympathized.

"You got this, Ing, you're almost out. You can do it. And boy, does it feel *amazing*!" Jon said, ecstatically. As usual, he was right.

Finally, the morning came. I was cleared to leave! I paused and looked at the space I had occupied 24/7 for fifteen and a half days. I captured a video of these two rooms and, before closing the door that I had been waiting to step through, looked back and wondered about the next person who would occupy them. I entered the hallway for the first time since my arrival. I jogged to the elevator with my suitcases, went down to the basement, and caught a car service immediately to Ma and Ba's place in New Taipei City. I kept the window down to stick part of my face out so I could feel the air and smell the city. I felt a burst of giddiness, a spike of hormones release from the euphoria of being set free. Jon was right, this *was* amazing.

I pulled up to the entrance of my parents' apartment complex. I collected my luggage and belongings and bolted down the hall to the elevator. I selected their floor, texted I was coming up, and burst through their unlocked door. Jon greeted me and we hugged tightly.

"You made it, loves," he said.

Seeing Jon reminded me of us exploring the city as kids, which I felt compelled to do now. *Let's go explore and get out!* I had so much energy in my newfound liberation. And then I saw it out of the corner of my eye: the oxygen machine. Its repetitive, grinding sound drew our attention. Jon looked at the machine and back at me.

"Ba and Ma are in their room," he said in answer to my inquisitive expression.

After leaving my shoes and luggage at the front door, I followed the trail of the extended oxygen line to their room. I entered softly, so happy to finally arrive. I hugged Ba, who greeted me. Ma was asleep, but she was opening her eyes. I looked down at her lying in bed and rushed to her side.

"Ma Bao Bei," she whispered.

I responded with the same phrase back to her: "Mother dearest." I leaned in and kissed her forehead and went to hug her. I jolted when I felt her body. She had lost a significant amount of weight and was frailer than she had been in San Francisco. It was as if half of her body had disappeared.

I didn't recognize this version of her—emaciated, weak, and tired. I couldn't seem to catch up to my shock and the sensation that repeated each time I touched her. I was in disbelief and deeply concerned. She was fading.

I was also in shock that I was finally with her and our family after wanting to be there for so long. It took such a journey to be there, right in that moment. I stayed with her as she smiled and closed her eyes. In a few moments, I'd have a panicked, guttural reaction outside her room. But in that moment, it was me and Ma. I had made it. I shifted from quarantine-survival mode to high gear—taking care of Ma and being with family was what I was there to do.

AMIDST THE fast-paced demands of daily caretaking—cooking, shopping for food, cleaning, making tea, checking in how family members were doing, and caring for the patient—Ma and I began having a series of spontaneous, deep conversations during quiet moments.

Ma seemed to save up her energy for these talks that had a finality to them. One talk was about spiritual healing. Walking through each stage of my life, Ma would ask if I wanted healing for that period. I always responded yes. Fatigued, she'd continue. Periodically, she would apologize for the mistakes she and Ba had made as parents. I'd reassure her, and she'd continue. Ma loved the talking stick. But I knew this was something she wanted to do for me. I recorded that session, a whisper of her voice on my phone, which I haven't had the strength to listen to.

In a separate conversation, after I had brought her a cup of tea as she sat on the living room couch, I brought up how

I still struggled with deep sensitivity. Whenever my feelings were hurt or I perceived someone I loved was betraying or rejecting me, I fell into what felt like a deep emotional well. In this well, it was hard to reach me. I would immediately consider worst-case scenarios. In my planning for catastrophe, I'd end up in this spiral, which would leave me at the bottom of this metaphorical well.

The well was lonely, protective, and like a cage. In it, I was covered with microaggressions and experiences of discrimination, as if they were tangible. I felt overwhelmed by feeling misunderstood and had accepted that I'd always be an outsider, never belonging, always alone. The animated Pixar movie *Soul* does a fantastic recreation of this experience with the character named 22, who, upon feeling rejected, is found in a tornado vortex, lost, as she sits watching warped replays of tormenting scenes. My well was ancient and deep. Mentally climbing out of it was difficult and could take days.

I described the well to Ma. I watched as her facial expression changed. She softened but almost winced. Then her body stiffened, relaxed, and seemed to warm to me. I looked at her with active attention and picked up on the shift in her. I was as present as possible, waiting for her to speak.

"Bei. That well... is mine," she said.

I sat with what she had said. I had never considered that the well might not be my own creation. I continued to scan her facial expressions, then met her eyes. We were silent. She breathed with the loud ferocity of the oxygen tank working overtime. It was like a permanent tiara for the rim of her mouth and the bottom of her nose. The oxygen cord was translucent green and always appeared empty—as if nothing was flowing in the tubes, yet it provided invisible oxygen, what every human life needs to live. Ma focused on breathing. I started to wonder if that was all she was going to say. And I began to picture her as a young child digging this metaphorical well. Then as a young woman who used the well to escape, even to get some alone time. Maybe to self-punish. As an adult, she used the well to soothe her wounds of discrimination and disappointment. She longed for tenderness, acceptance, the feeling of being unconditionally loved—of being seen, heard, and valued. How had we never spoken about our shared well experiences before? How had we never talked about how we shared, even inherited, this pain? It was a mystery that was becoming incredibly clear. It was up to me to fill up the well and part ways with it for good.

Ma studied me as I sat with these thoughts and she calmed herself, closing her eyes as if comforted by the shift in my energy. She was handing me the task that she perhaps didn't have the strength or skills to do herself.

A few days passed following the same routine of caring for a loved one who is ill. You try to make your loved one comfortable, follow their energy and appetite, and move from one room to another depending on their mood. Again, Ma and I found ourselves on the living room couch and we started talking about mean-girl culture. I'm not sure what compelled me to share the story of what happened to me as a ten-year-old in the little barn, when the girls locked me in the stall and blasted me with a hose. I shared the story with Ma while Ba was in earshot, and I wasn't particularly emotional about it. In fact, I smirked about how odd that experience was now that I was an adult looking back on it. There was just so much space between my little-girl self and me as an adult. I knew the main bully felt badly about it. Years later, she'd reached out and apologized, which I accepted, but that was the extent of my engagement with her. But Ma, who never got to hear the story when I was a little girl, seemed to take it as raw, current, vivid—and extremely painful. She started shaking, and because she was so frail, it meant her entire body was quaking in its force.

"Ma, are you okay?!" I said as I held her.

Her body erupted into tears, which poured out of her eyes. She was bawling on my behalf. There were no words, just gasping for air, crying. I watched her, wondering what it would have been like if I had gone home that day and told her what had happened. Would she have hugged me, protected me, explained what bullying was? Would she have explained her own experiences with bullying and othering from racism and sexism, and other forms of discrimination?

Thirty years or so later, here she was, bawling on my behalf with half her lung capacity, as I held her closely and assured her, "Ma, I'm okay. It was a long time ago. Thank you for crying for me. I am healed from that experience, I'm okay."

I felt badly for sharing a story that made her hurt so deeply. She had no words afterwards. Just fatigue. I kept soothing her. I pictured placing a beautiful horse in her lungs to help her traverse the landscape cancer had created; burned and damaged from chemo, radiation, immunotherapy, effusion—it was a war zone. I pictured the horse trying to graze among the damaged brush, a pink storm filling her lung cavity. It looked like an apocalypse. I mentally pushed the image of the horse as a comforting life force in her wound. I looked at Ma. We shared pain from our similar, yet different experiences. We had reached the height of our mother-daughter connection. Our experiences came out of a similar struggle around who belongs and who does not, who is valued and who is not, who is heard and who is not. We were Blackie in his stall, tending to our wounds but no longer alone.

AFTER FIVE WEEKS in Taipei, I reluctantly returned to the United States and work life. However, it did feel good to reunite with Courtney and our recently adopted puppy. When I landed back in the US, I felt different. I felt a deepening, a wisdom growing strong within me. And a yearning for Ma. Her decline made me acutely aware of and grateful for my health. I was grateful to still have life to live and choices to make about what that might entail. No longer confined to two quarantine rooms or my parents' apartment, I went for nature walks and observed the balance of life and death happening in nature. I was grateful for the support of my wife and family, and the connections I had with Ma. It was just in time. My visa was single entry, and the borders were about to close again.

Jon remained in Taipei for another month, working from my parents' apartment by himself. Ma and Ba had gone to the hospital, which they did every three weeks, for her immunotherapy treatment, but this time the oncologist

Our experiences came out of a similar struggle around who belongs and who does not, who is valued and who is not, who is heard and who is not.

found complications with her pleural effusion. Her frail chest had to be punctured to release fluid from a large, gauged tube. She was in pain and wanted to be released to go home, but the fluid kept coming. Then she caught an infection in the hospital and ran a fever. She needed a high dose of antibiotics that required daily monitoring. Since this was during peak COVID pandemic, only Ba could stay with Ma in the hospital. And so, Jon waited for them in hopes that they'd be able to return home each week, which never came. Eventually, he took a PCR test twenty-four hours before his flight home and the hospital was kind enough to accept his negative test result so that he could visit Ma and Ba for one hour before heading to the airport. I listened to his retelling of the fleeting yet intimate connection that one hour provided, not knowing that a similar experience would be in my future.

Ma and Ba were at the beginning of a month-long hospital stay. More infections, fevers, treatments, and fluids to release. Every hospital stay was a COVID risk. The virus was spreading across the island. And then, special entry visa applications were on hold for almost ten months, barring Jon and I from entry. We spent every day on the phone with Ma and Ba and monitored news of the border and when special entry visa applications would re-open. Courtney watched these daily interactions and sat with me in the metaphorical rollercoaster of a waiting room.

Ma finished her thesis, graduated top of her class, and received her degree in between hospital visits. Her determination was profound. However, shortly after we celebrated over Zoom, Jon and I received an unexpected call from

Ba. The death-star tumor had punctured Ma's windpipe, asphyxiating her. She needed an emergency surgery. He had just signed paperwork in Chinese that indicated she had a 50-percent chance of survival. Ba was in shock, freaking out, crying, and feeling defeated, terrified, and alone. I caught the wave of his energy and immediately began heavy research into how to get to Taipei for a family emergency, for a dying parent.

Ma survived the surgery odds and remained in the hospital with Ba. Two weeks later came a timely miracle—it was announced that special entry visa applications had re-opened. That day, I shipped off my passport with the completed application, prepaid return envelope, and a check to TECO.

While I waited for my special entry application to be processed, I joined a grief group. I had such strong anticipatory grief and fear about losing Ma, which felt within arm's reach. I thought about how Ma handled her own mother's passing with such dignity and devotion. I thought about looking down at her in a casket surrounded by flowers and shed a tear. It was an honor to be part of this matriarchal lineage. I knew soon we would be faced with having to say our goodbyes.

Three weeks later, the mail arrived and inside—finally—was the returned envelope with my passport and visa. The next day, I arranged a PCR test and booked both my flight and quarantine hotel—a different hotel than the last one. I don't think I can ever return to either hotel. I held Courtney and our puppy close. My last meal before the trip was pasta with meat sauce, ahead of the daily fried rice that awaited.

That meal reminded me of Nai Nai and my outburst, its aftermath, and how I felt like a lion roaring, demanding now not to be respected but that cancer not take away my mom.

On the long, fourteen-hour flight to Taipei, I thought of all the provisions I packed for my second hotel-quarantine journey. I thought of Ma recovering from her emergency surgery. What state would I find her and my father in? I thought of Courtney at home caring for our dog and maintaining life in a home we had recently moved into in Sausalito, California. We had found our dream home and sold our San Francisco property. So much had happened within these eleven months, yet being apart from Ma during this time felt like an anxious eternity of waiting for news and an opportunity to get back to her. I looked out the plane window and tried to wrap my head around the concept of being in the air, cutting through clouds to finally get to Ma.

I braced myself for the slightly different quarantine experience that awaited me. It wasn't my first rodeo, so to speak, but it was, to my relief, shortened to twelve days. Given the status of a hospitalized parent, I applied to have daily, one-hour hospital visits. Theses visits weren't guaranteed—they required the local police and CDC health representative to coordinate a PCR test at one of the local hospitals. Once the hospital approved the negative test result, the police would arrange a quarantine taxi to escort me to and from the test. I'd be sprayed down before getting into the vehicle and dropped off to navigate an onslaught of outdoor lines and clinics. Each day, I scrambled to figure out in my broken Chinese if I was in the right line for the right type of COVID test. Half the time, I wasn't, and I risked getting exposed or getting an antigen test instead of the required PCR one. Each of these experiences took hours—and even if it was momentarily refreshing to be outdoors, the chaos of the experience and the process was stressful.

Once I returned to the basement of the hotel, I was sprayed down again before entering the elevator taking me up to my room. I waited for the police to call me with my test results. If they were negative and it wasn't too late, the officer could coordinate a short visit with the hospital director. A quarantine taxi would be dispatched on my behalf. If I was fortunate, by dinnertime I'd be escorted to the hospital to be with Ma and Ba for an hour.

It took four days before one of these hospital visits came to fruition. And I was so relieved when it finally did. I had a small window where I could order a meal or treat to bring with me for my parents. Ba said that Ma was craving lasagna, one of her favorites. He warned me that Ma had sores in and over her mouth post-surgery. She could barely taste or eat. Swallowing hurt. She was frustrated and desperate to be released from the hospital. I shared her desperation. I ordered the lasagna and waited for it to arrive, lulling my mind into that space where patience fights disassociation and meets acceptance for what's to come.

Lasagna in tow, I met Ba at the hospital entrance where the quarantine taxi dropped me off. We embraced. I was so thankful for him. He walked me into the hospital and the staff waved at us. Ba had spent so much time at the hospital that they knew him—he was a regular. We went up to the elevator, and he selected the floor. I started to feel anxious and worried. I had waited almost a year to get to this point. I walked the few feet left towards Ma's hospital room. I was finally about to be reunited with her.

I entered her room, feeling as though I was entering another dimension. A staff person was cleaning her bedpan. I ignored it and all it symbolized. Instead, I went to hug Ma immediately as she lay motionless in her bed. I excitedly told her I brought lasagna and that I hoped she'd enjoy it. She gave me a weak smile, careful not to crack the many dark scabs on her mouth, but her eyes lit up. Ba helped her sit up. She was much frailer, which I didn't think possible, and down to ninety pounds. I shuddered, held in my aching cry, and focused on keeping her spirits lifted.

The act of sitting up tired her. She looked down and her tiny hand gripped the railing of the bed. She looked back at me, her eyes steady, hungry for the lasagna. I quickly opened the box—the lasagna did look delicious. I cut a small bite and brought it up to her lips. She clung to the fork as she maneuvered her mouth over the precious pasta. She closed her eyes, made a few chews, and tried to swallow. She squinted and made a pained expression. Her eyes opened full of disappointment. She cried, which took a tremendous amount of her resources. The food hurt going down and she couldn't taste what she wanted so badly to enjoy. Ma not being able to eat was devastating to us both, two rice buckets who loved eating. I had failed, and I could no longer hold back my tears.

Ba took the box of lasagna. "Ing, I'm starving." He consumed the lasagna in what seemed like a few bites, and I saw his caretaking fatigue, how rare it was for him to enjoy something special for himself to eat. I hadn't thought of what he might want to enjoy, which made me shed even more tears. Ba had suffered, too. Ma became thirsty, and I watched as Ba used a pipette to bring water to her mouth. She was in rough shape and moody. She demanded to go home. I held her hand for most of the minutes I had left, watching her suffer through her unease and finally, rest. Periodically, she'd gently tap or rub an index finger or thumb over my hand. In wonder, I compared how large my hand looked to the delicate, lean fingers I held. I looked away, up at the monitor, watching her heartbeat repeat the letter Y, which echoed in my head: *Why, why, why, why?*

Out of nowhere, the timer went off and I had to leave. It was so abrupt, so daunting. I told Ma and Ba I'd see them the next day and Ba walked me down to where my quarantine taxi awaited my arrival.

"Ba, this isn't looking good."

He was quiet and simply nodded.

"Home hospice could be really tough. Will you—will we—be alright?" I asked, concerned.

I COULDN'T RETURN the next day, nor the following. COVID cases spiked, and the hospitals were so overwhelmed by people trying to get tests that lines wrapped around multiple blocks. I could *not* afford to get COVID, which would jeopardize my chances of seeing Ma and Ba and also mean spending many more weeks at a medical facility. These chaotic adventures left me helpless and pacing in my hotel cell, waiting for the police to ring with better news.

As my days in quarantine ended, Ba signed paperwork to release Ma from the hospital, opting for home hospice. She was done with the hospital but was also asking when they could begin treatment again. *Ma, there will be no more treatments if you are in hospice.* I knew she knew that, but she was entering a phase where she was starting to hallucinate. I had done preliminary research on the common signs of a person nearing death. Looking at Ma, I could see that death would be a release for her. She was in pain, and they were prescribing her morphine and fentanyl. The cancer was continuing to grow past her esophagus and into her shoulder, making a beeline to the surface of her skin. A small dome appeared on the surface of her right shoulder as the cancer drilled tirelessly through what little muscle she had.

It dawned on me that we were entering Ma's final chapter, and I texted Jon. He was still waiting for his passport and visa to arrive, which had somehow gotten lost in the mail; he was helpless and scared. It was my turn to reassure him, he would get here in time.

Finally, Jon's passport arrived, and he was on a flight to Taipei just as the quarantine hotel time was reduced in May 2022 to seven days. We were amazed by that fortuitous timing. Jon would be out of quarantine sooner than expected, making up time lost.

While he was in the air, I was released from my hotel and arrived just after Ba and Ma got home. Ma was hallucinating; she couldn't walk on her own but kept trying to and would fall. Ba was frantically trying to reason with her. She was restless. It took some convincing and practice to lift her to use the commode next to her bed—it was too challenging to assist her to the ensuite bathroom nearby.

One moment, Ma would cry out to go outside and leave the apartment; the next, she'd lie in bed so still and immobile I'd have to check to make sure she was still breathing. And then, she started talking to people we could not see. She had entire conversations with old friends and neighbors. She'd describe seeing young kids and animals visiting her in vibrant colors that filled the room. I treated her hallucinations as opportunities to engage with her and asked her to describe the world she saw and was possibly entering. She was somewhere in the in-between: halfway with us and halfway in her own world, mesmerized by what she saw in her hallucinations until a jolt of pain and discomfort brought her back into the harsh reality of her broken, physical experience. We managed her pain medication as best we could. Eventually it would take effect, and she'd sleep. We navigated these states to make her as comfortable as possible, while we ourselves lived in a state of constant anxiety, fear, and helplessness. At one point, she looked at me very clearly. I used the moment to tell her, "Ma Bao Bei, I love you."

"T'en ai," she responded, looking at me. That was how she said *I love you so much it hurts*. She offered me a tiny smile that seemed to take great effort and, in a whisper, said, "Thank you for coming, bei."

I hold that sweet exchange close to my heart.

As we waited for Jon to arrive, I continued to pipette water, room-temperature tea, and protein drinks to her to battle her significant weight loss. We tried offering her oatmeal, apple sauce, and ice cream with varying degrees of success. She was barely eating. Ba and I worked as a team. I wasn't allowed to leave the apartment for a week after quarantine and my cell phone was tracked, so I'd watch Ma as Ba went grocery shopping, picked up meds, retrieved hospital records, and ran important errands. I took Ma's temperature, talked to her, lay next to her, turned her over to prevent more bed sores from forming, and tried not to heave or bawl whenever her clothes rolled up and I caught a glimpse of her emaciated body.

By the time Jon got out of his quarantine hotel seven days later, I had gotten pretty used to helping Ma pee, wiping her down, feeding her, and administering meds with Ba. The dining table was a flurry of meds and medical supplies. She had a new wound we needed to clean and monitor, and Ba was researching how to get a hospice nurse to help for an hour or two a day. He was thinking ahead for when I'd eventually return home.

Ba thanked me immensely for coming. "Ing, I couldn't have done this without you. The timing was perfect." I felt so good that I was there to help. It wasn't out of my desire to be a dutiful daughter. It was out of love and finality.

When Jon arrived, he looked at Ma, and I saw shock hit his system. I walked him through our care routine, but he could barely follow—he was so overwhelmed. Ma was his confidante, and he was her favorite. He went to her bedside and just lay next to her, cuddling her. Ba and I let them be. This was going to be hard on all of us, but I watched the impact it was having on my brother, knowing that after all the anticipatory grief we had lived through, now—here with us—death shared the room we occupied and was planning to enter center stage at any moment.

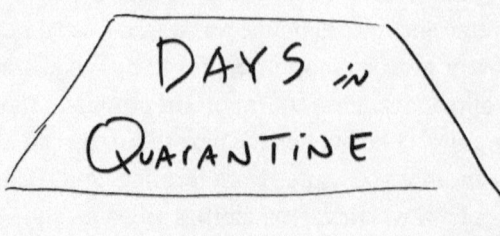

top Crossing off completed days in quarantine.

bottom Jon and I finally arrive to be with Ma after quarantine.

In our anticipatory grief, we remember when Ma was healthy and we were all together, with her at the center.

THE PHOENIX

IT WAS 3 A.M. when I woke up with a strange feeling. I checked my phone. Ba had called and left a voice message. I put the phone up to my ear and listened. Every word of his message spun my chest into spasms, gasping for air: "It grieves me to say that your beautiful mother has left this world."

Ma died a day before turning sixty-seven.

I felt a phantom umbilical cord wrapped around my neck. It was as if the moment I entered the world through Ma's body was now overlayed with the moment her soul left the world. I continued gasping and felt like I was suffocating. But, this time, there was no physical cord to wrestle away to freedom. I held on to the feeling; it connected me to her through time. It connected me to her physical trauma, when cancer broke into her air passageway, and she asphyxiated. She spent two years living with an oxygen machine, its brightly colored lime tubes following her every step. It brought me to her final moments, where oxygen left the parts of her brain that kept her alive. In breath do us part.

The moment passed and I was again horrified by the shock of the news. I was angry—cancer had pushed it too far—and now neither it nor Ma had survived. I was devastated and felt desperate despair. I pictured all that Ma and I would miss, her elder years, all the future scenes we could have spent together, now taken from us. I wanted to continue to connect and build on our relationship, to share all that we had missed and all that we could have grown together. There would be no additional time. She had left this physical world, and I would never see her again.

I sat on the edge of my bed, howling. Courtney kneeled on the floor and held on to my knees, guiding me like a shaman through what she recalled from her own experience of her father's passing. I looked at her through my pain and desperation, the yearning I felt. Despite my anguish, I felt grateful for her expertise and understanding while I writhed in the rebelliousness and cruelty of grief as it transformed into its purest form, ignited by permanent loss.

"Try to breathe, babe. Take a breath, love. *Breathe*. I know, I know."

The tears oozed out of my eyes, hot and thick, as my body pulsated, emulating the physical sensation of losing oxygen—trying to link me back to Ma.

Ma had held on for a month past what every hospice professional thought possible. By that time, Jon and I had returned home. Even though I kept telling Ma it was okay to let go, she held on. And part of me wondered if it was because we were there. Our jobs, our lives, our partners awaited our return. The morning of my flight, which I had rescheduled and pushed out, I kissed her forehead. "Goodbye, Ma. I love you." And I knew that it was my last goodbye. I made peace with that. I had done everything I came here to do. Saying goodbye, having heard her say she loved me, being with her in moments she was relatively conscious—all of that was a gift.

After Jon departed shortly after me, Ba had about a week of caretaking solo, which was terribly challenging. Twice during the middle of the night, Ma maneuvered around the barriers of her bed, as if trying to free herself from her stall, and fell. Both times she was rushed to the hospital. Ba was desperate to sleep and realized Ma needed full-time care. He couldn't reason with her; she took everything as a child would hearing the word "no" too many times. In this in-between mental state, she received Ba's pleas for her to stay in bed as scolding. Just like the hour I was granted during my quarantine hospital visits, the hour provided by the visiting hospice nurse wasn't enough. Ba agreed with us that it was time to call the hospice hospital and secure a room for Ma. As he waited, he arranged for local family members to say their goodbyes.

The day the hospice hospital called with a room for Ma and dispatched an ambulance to come get her, Ba noticed something different. Ma's head had tilted to the side. She was drooling, her body following the weight of her skull as if diving into water. He checked her oxygen levels, and they were dangerously low, even though the oxygen machine was on full blast. He was by Ma's side the whole time as hospital workers collected her, placed her in the ambulance, and drove her to the hospital. After they arrived, they waited for a room, but Ma hadn't improved. Ba expressed this to the nurse and they examined her. A room was assigned, and Ba waited for the doctor to arrive.

By the time the doctor showed up, Ba felt that Ma had already left. He had listened to her breathing change. It was slow and distant, with long gaps where a breath wasn't taken, until... there were no more inhales that followed. Ba stared out at the window, pained by the reality of what had just transpired, and he couldn't turn around. As the doctor walked in, he asked her to check whether Ma had passed. The doctor checked. She paused before confirming. Ma had left her body for good. Ba expressed relief that neither of us had to witness what was left of her frail body turning an eerie shade of pale gray. That he had to witness this alone fills me with sorrow.

BEFORE I LEFT TAIWAN, I went through my parents' belongings and gave away or got rid of as much as I could to assist Ba with the aftermath of Ma's passing. We knew it was likely that he'd move back to the States. Ba had plenty to attend to after Ma's death and I wanted to make the upcoming transition as easy as possible without me there in person. I went through all of Ma's things during the long hours she lay in bed sleeping. I bagged up her shoes, sorted her clothes and jewelry, cleaned, and repacked everything. I knew that once we left, we wouldn't be allowed to re-enter the country due to COVID and single-entry visa restrictions.

Ba wanted Ma's body cremated so that he could place half her ashes in an urn in Taipei and bring the rest with him for a burial in New Jersey. However, in Taiwan,

We are all part of the
same life force,
yet we learn to divide
ourselves into groups:
who belongs, who is
different, who is superior,
who is the outsider.

cremation isn't a full cremation. In their process, most of Ma's charred skeleton remained scattered across a small dusting of ash. Given the desire to place her in two separate urns, her entire skeleton was carefully divided in half.

I thought about how poetic that was—for Ma's remains to be split in half. I was someone who was regarded as half-and-half my entire life. Here, in Ma's death, she, too, experienced that bifurcation. It was as if she was finally experiencing what it was like for her kids to grow up mixed-race in a world full of division, feeling dehumanized by the limitations and harm of categorization. We are all part of the same life force, yet we learn to divide ourselves into groups: who belongs, who is different, who is superior, who is the outsider. I've found that never truly belonging has given me great comfort in being the outsider and navigating the in-between, and all the insights that perspective affords. I reflected on how I had navigated so many iterations of the spotlight, and how I finally had a version of it in my professional life that aligned with my truth and my power. Ma's divided remains were a nod to the cultures we both navigated: Taiwan, where it started and ended; and New Jersey, where we spent most of our time together as a family.

After Ma died, neither Jon nor I could return to the country. And so, Ba organized Ma's memorial service in Taipei as I organized her service stateside. In Taipei, each family member was directed to pick up one of my mother's bones using a pair of tongs and place it in her urn. Ba almost vomited, but he held it together and followed the formality, picking up what looked like a vertebra. After the whirlwind of executing a memorial service, Ba packed up the things he'd take with him to the US, selling and giving away everything that didn't fit in his suitcases. It was like he was back in the 2008 recession, but this time, he was alone. After saying his goodbyes to his friends, family, and a life that was always tethered to Ma, he boarded the long plane ride home with her remaining half.

Ba moved back to the fifty-five-and-up community in New Jersey that he had once lived in with Ma. He wanted to be in a familiar place, but this might have been a bit *too* familiar and, simultaneously, strangely foreign. This had been the house of someone else, a woman who died, and here we were, standing idlily in her living room.

When we met Ba at his new apartment, we moved Ma's remains into her US-based urn. Feeling the weight of half of Ma's bones—hearing them tumble into a stone vessel inscribed with her name and life span—was surreal. It felt impossible. How was it that Ma's remains, what was left of her, sounded just like heavy items in a drying machine? Tumbling, as if mixed with dirt and sand, falling into a vessel that we sealed shut. We stood there, wrestling with our limited abilities to process this harsh reality as it sat there. Ma was dead, she was gone, and we were left with this container to bury. It made no sense. And so, we stood, stunned by the permanence before us, grief gushing out like a river from our souls, silently roaring. If it weren't for the funeral and celebration of life that we had to get to, we might have stood there, forever shocked and numb.

Ba said that without Ma, his life was like a poster with a big gaping hole in the center. Forty-three years of marriage and friendship was gone in a blink of an eye. He let guilt enter and questioned himself: Couldn't he have done more as her caretaker, pushed for other treatments? Jon and I consoled him as we navigated our own cluster of guilt, pain, grief, and loss. I looked at my father, then my brother. Suddenly, I realized that I was the only remaining female in our nuclear family. The nuclear family Ma always wanted to perfect and outwardly project. Without her, we were exposed in our imperfection, turned inward in our pain. I felt desperately alone without her. It was a moment that had me gasping for air.

I ORGANIZED NOT ONE but two celebrations of life for Ma. The first was with my friends and chosen family in California. We served trays of lasagna in Ma's honor and played her favorite songs from ABBA, the Bee Gees, and Air Supply. We projected a photo album of Ma on our TV screen. I almost cancelled the memorial that morning because my grief felt so overwhelming and I didn't think I could see my group of family and friends so soon. Courtney reminded me that having close friends witness this truth was part of the healing process. And so, we welcomed our guests into our home filled with our grief.

Through a steady flow of tears, I gave a short speech about Ma. It was helpful being surrounded by loved ones, my community, and their gifts and flowers—but all I wanted was for Ma to be back. I pictured her being one of the persons at the door, healthy and laughing. Telling me it was all a bad nightmare, that she'd just been on a long trip and had, in fact, decided to move near us! "Surprise!" she'd say, with a sassy dance, and place her hands behind her head in two peace signs that looked like rabbit ears, feigning innocence. But she never arrived.

As each person hugged me and said their sweet words of support before taking their leave, I looked around at the flowers and begged them to stay alive for as long as they could. I couldn't bear to see a living thing die.

THE SECOND CELEBRATION of life I arranged was for the day of Ma's funeral service in New Jersey. When we stood lifeless in front of her urn in what was now Ba's living room, I realized we had to get going. We had the funeral to get to.

It was a bitterly cold fall morning on the day of the funeral. A combination of family and friends joined us at the plot where Ma's urn would be buried. I looked around and saw cousins, aunts, and uncles, as well as former bandmates, friends, and those who knew me and Ma dearly. Parixit and Dane were there, honoring me during this tender moment. Their presence reminded me that I was loved and made me reflect on my journey—as a horse rider, a musician, a brave and courageous woman. A warrior. A person who loves and has the capacity to forgive. A person determined to live her truth despite the pressure of society and family. I felt seen and respected. All these years, they had been the witnesses of my life. They were family.

Ba read a passage from the Bible. Practicing it, he had never gotten through it without bawling and breaking down. Now he got through it with the steadiness he had hoped for. We were proud of him. He honored Ma to his fullest, just as she had for Nai Nai. He called Jon and I over to sprinkle dirt into Ma's grave, its mouth full with her urn. My spine felt numb, like an old machine struggling to turn on, and I hesitated to move. Although it was cripplingly cold, warmth flushed into my face. A pool of tears hovered under my eyes as I exchanged glances with Courtney and let the dirt slide past my fingers, sprinkling onto the surface of Ma's remains in tiny thuds.

Hearing the dirt fall reminded me of the patter of rain when Courtney and I heard news that Ma's cancer had come back. Watching the dirt fall reminded me of coming home after my days at the horse barn, when Ma would tell me to throw my laundry in the machine and shower before dinner. I thought about that moment Ma spoke to Ziggy, my horse, before getting in the ring, calming him as her way of supporting me. I shook through each memory and managed to return to Courtney's side. She pulled me close and leaned her head into my neck and shoulder, bawling. After the ceremony, I hugged Ba and Jon, our small broken nucleus. But we had each other, and shared what left us with broken hearts.

It was time to head to Ma's memorial service, which I'd booked at her favorite fancy restaurant, the Ryland Inn, months prior. I handled all the logistics, selected the menu, and sent out invitations, bringing both sides of my family together to honor Ma—many of whom hadn't seen one another in decades. My wife put together an expanded playlist and Jon set up a projector to replay our photo album. Our aunts coordinated and arranged the flowers. They had rented a large home so that family could stay under one roof, eat meals together, and connect as we navigated between the various events. It gave everyone a space to show up and honor Ma, and witness us picking up the pieces of our old lives as we crawled, reluctantly, into this next chapter.

AT THE RYLAND INN, Courtney and I stepped into host mode and made sure everything was ready and guests felt welcomed. It was a beautiful setup. I touched the cursive font on the menu and thought Ma would have been pleased. I pictured her looking at the faces of every family member feeling loved, adored, and respected. I thought about the journey ahead for all of us she had left behind, our grief and connection, our shared love and remembrance.

A displayed photo caught a moment of Ma's mannerisms, which ignited laughter, tenderness, and tears. I felt Ma telling me that she would show up in my dreams and reach out to me. Her photos served as a reminder of how strong and determined her spirit was and the love she had for us, too. The warm glow of the fireplace danced across our faces, and I could feel Ma's presence. For the first time, I felt a sliver of hope—that our connection might extend beyond death's dimension. As we celebrated her life that night, I thought about the card she gave Courtney and me on her last day in San Francisco after completing her internship, which we had framed in my office. In it, she wrote:

I think our ultimate goal is to live a good life to the very end. We have purposes larger than ourselves. Faced with my own mortality, I begin to understand the meaning of courage.

Choosing to live your truth and be who you are is the most rebellious act against fear of rejection, disappointment, shame, and abandonment.

"Courage is strength in the face of knowledge of what is to be feared or hoped."

We seek out the truth of what is to be hoped, and act on the truth we find to shape our stories. For the human being, life is meaningful because it's a story. And in stories, endings matter.

I shall go on to write and create the remaining few chapters of my life. Hopefully, it'll be a story worth reading for my children and generations to come.

How prophetic she was. She quotes a line from Atul Gawande's book, *Being Mortal*, which we had read together years prior. It was as if Ma knew then that she would die. Death was not something she liked to talk about, yet, in this goodbye card, it was all there. It reminded me of what I had learned in my life thus far that I could share with others: Choosing to live your truth and be who you are is the most rebellious act against fear of rejection, disappointment, shame, and abandonment. To choose fear comes at great cost, to you and others. Choosing your truth comes with liberation, with the possibility to change the dynamics of cultural and familial pressure placed upon you and those closest to you.

The morning after Ma's funeral and celebration of life event, I woke up with a tingling sensation, picturing a stunning phoenix circling above the house we were staying in. I smiled, convinced that it was Ma's spirit, thanking us for honoring her and sharing her love.

Courtney's arm was around me as she slept soundly. I turned and looked out the window. To my surprise, snow had lightly dusted the grounds during the night and the sun was shining—its glittery landscape sparkling like crystals. *Sun shining on morning snow.* The name Ma had given me. I knew this was a symbolic gift from her. I smiled feeling showered in her love. She was free and she was everywhere.

"Ma Bao Bei," I called out to her in my mind. "I love you."

top I woke up after Ma's celebration of life to the sun shining on the morning snow. Thank you, Ma.

bottom At Ma's funeral service in New Jersey, Ba, Jon, and I embrace.

top Ma is free.

bottom The thank-you card Ma wrote to Courtney and me, capturing her wisdom.

ACKNOWLEDGMENTS

THIS BOOK would not have been possible without the encouragement and support of my wife, Courtney Howard, who didn't hesitate to invest in a writing coach and hybrid publisher to get my story out into the world. Courtney bore witness to what became a yearlong process, encouraging me to keep going, reading drafts, and creating the conditions for me to breathe life into my memoir.

My life story wouldn't be possible without both Ba and my brother, Jon. They bore deeply into my manuscript, offered feedback, and fact-checked on my behalf. They questioned and probed, encouraged, and challenged me. They also tirelessly searched and scanned the higher resolution photos that appear after each chapter. Thank you, loves.

Thank you, former colleague and fellow author Regina Lawless for introducing me to writing coach Stacy Ennis, who taught, guided, and supported me throughout the book-writing process. Stacy became not only my book shaman but my friend. She helped me find my writing voice and encouraged me to reach out to my dream editor, Katie

Gee Salisbury, author of the book *Not Your China Doll*. I wanted to have a mixed-race, Asian female–dominated team; to my delight, Katie not only responded to my inquiry but, after our introductory call, agreed to join my team as substantive editor. As a mixed-race author, Katie saw and understood my story, challenging me to go deeper in the details that were tough but necessary to share and write.

Stacy introduced me to Page Two publishers, and after reading the first draft of my manuscript, co-owner Jesse Finkelstein called me. She felt my story, could picture my Ma, and believed that readers would connect to my journey of identity, loss, forgiveness, and living my truth. After I signed with Page Two, four important women joined my team: Carmen Ho, my fantastic project manager; Erin Parker, my copyeditor, who expertly helped bring my manuscript over the finish line; Taysia Louie, my creative design lead; and Adrineh Der-Boghossian, my proofreader.

Thank you to my former design colleague and hapa-sister Lisa Whitsitt-Takata, who not only dove into my manuscript as one of my beta-reader champions but brainstormed book cover ideas to capture the essence of my story. Our ideations inspired me to reach out to the incredibly talented illustrator Hanna Barczyk. I've been a fan of Hanna's beautiful and powerful work for years—it is truly an honor to have her illustrate the cover of my book and to connect with my story.

Thank you to my vocal coach and fellow author Denise Woods, who coached me to narrate my story for the recorded audio edition by Twin Flames Studios. And thank you to my PR representative, Taryn Hennebicque, who skillfully amplified my book prior to launch.

A special thank-you to my beta readers, who provided initial feedback on my first draft: Lisa Whitsitt-Takata, Doris Caçoilo, Parixit Davé, Drea Collaço, Kathryn Baxter, Tania Goulart, Kendra Shimmell, Wyatt Starosta, Hanako Olmer, Aisha Fukushima, Tina Richards, Janet Freeman, and Diana Howard. An honorable mention to Courtney and her sister, Brit Howard, who came up with the proposed book title, *Half Pony and the Rice Bucket*, inspired after reading my manuscript. Their creative title is a noteworthy undercurrent of the book.

And to my beautiful mother, Hu Kuo-Ying, Judy Hu Dahl, Ma Bao Bei—t'en ai.

SUN SHINING ON MORNING SNOW

陶雪晴

AUTHOR'S NOTE

WRITING THIS MEMOIR, I followed many fascinating paths to learn more about the history of female soldiers in China, artists like Adrian Piper, and other interesting subjects. If you, too, would like to dive deeper, the resources I consulted are a good start.

They include the following:

- Najoua Chetioui's article "Female Soldiers Throughout Chinese History" (europeanguanxi.com/post/female-soldiers-throughout-chinese-history)

- *Autumn Gem: A Documentary on Modern China's First Feminist,* written and directed by Rae Chang (autumn-gem.com)

- Nathan Ma's article "Adrian Piper's *Catalysis* Taught Me How to Resist Everyday Racism (elephant.art/nathan-ma-on-adrian-pipers-catalysis/)

- The Hammer Museum's description of Piper's installation *Cornered* (hammer.ucla.edu/take-it-or-leave-it/art/cornered)

ABOUT THE AUTHOR

INGRID HU DAHL is an author, speaker, and leadership coach. She is the founder of her own coaching and consulting business, dedicated to empowering the next generation of leaders. With over two decades of experience in learning and development, she specializes in leadership, inclusion, and belonging, bringing her expertise to a wide range of industries, from corporate and media to nonprofit and social justice organizations.

A TEDx speaker and a founding member of the Willie Mae Rock Camp in Brooklyn, Ingrid has a lifelong passion for amplifying underrepresented voices. She has performed in multiple touring bands and has written, filmed, and directed two short films exploring identity, representation, and the mixed-race experience. Through her work, she shares stories of living in the in-between with curiosity and empathy, fostering deeper connections and cross-cultural understanding.

PHOTO: LAUREN TABAK

Ingrid is certified by the International Coaching Federation and the Center for Creative Leadership. She is a global lecturer and speaker, an advisory board member for the Institute for Women's Leadership at Rutgers University, and a former board member of the Bay Area Girls Rock Camp. She lives in Sausalito, California, with her wife, Courtney, and their dog, Palo Santo.

Choosing to live your truth and be who you are is the most rebellious act against fear of rejection, disappointment, shame, and abandonment. To choose fear comes at great cost, to you and others. Choosing your truth comes with liberation, with the possibility to change the dynamics of cultural and familial pressure placed upon you and those closest to you.

SUN SHINING ON MORNING SNOW

陶雪晴

CONNECT WITH THE AUTHOR

WAYS TO ENGAGE

You can invite me to speak at your event, podcast, conference, offsite, whether in person or virtually for an inspiring keynote or an engaging fireside chat. I provide discounts when a bulk purchase of books is included.

I love joining heritage-month events focused on women's history, Asian (API), Pride, and mixed-race recognition moments throughout the year.

Bring me in to brainstorm, solution, design, facilitate, and lead workshops related to identity, leadership, and/or inclusion.

Related to leadership, inclusion, and big life moments, I offer one-on-one and group or team coaching and consulting for you and your teams to thrive—especially in moments that require courage and bravery.

Share my memoir with your community, department, team, or organization. I love it when my memoir is selected for book clubs. Contact me to for bulk purchases and special offers.

Share my memoir with anyone who is experiencing loss or difficulty belonging, who might be clashing with family or social expectations, who is coming out and feeling alone. Maybe you have a mixed-race family member who could be inspired to share more of their experience after reading my book. Maybe you might converse differently with people like me after hearing my story.

Want to spread the word by writing a review? I encourage you to write a review on whichever book retailer site you prefer. Thank you for putting your perspective out there. Sharing how my book impacted you inspires other readers to connect with my story and, hopefully, share their own. May we continue to connect and relate across difference in the physical world and the in-between.

HOW TO REACH ME

- hello@ingridhudahl.com
- @ingridhudahl
- @ingridhudahl
- sunshiningonmorningsnow.com
- ingridhudahl.com

www.ingramcontent.com/pod-product-compliance
Lightning Source LLC
Chambersburg PA
CBHW020518080526
44583CB00013B/647